AN ACCOUNT OF

WITCHCRAFT IN SCOTLAND.

A Historical Account of the Belief in Witchcraft in Scotland

Charles Kirkpatrick Sharpe

Kennedy & Boyd
an imprint of
Zeticula
57 St Vincent Crescent
Glasgow
G3 8NQ
Scotland.

http://www.kennedyandboyd.co.uk
admin@kennedyandboyd.co.uk

This edition Copyright © Zeticula 2011

ISBN-13 978-1-84921-064-5
All rights reserved. No part of this publication may be reproduced, stored in a retrieval system, or transmitted in any form or by any means, electronic, mechanical, photocopying, recording or otherwise, without the prior permission of the publishers.

EDITORIAL NOTE.

In the year 1819 Charles Kirkpatrick Sharpe edited from manuscript the work now commonly-known as Law's "Memorialls." Though now a standard work, and often quoted by historical writers, it had not been printed prior to the above-named date. The title in full runs as follows:—"Memorialls; or the Memorable Things that fell out Within this Island of Brittain from 1638 to 1684. By the Rev. Mr. Robert Law." In the preface to the "Memorialls" Mr. Sharpe says regarding the manuscript:—"The MS. from which the 'Memorialls' have been printed is not in the handwriting of the author. Transcribed with extreme inaccuracy by some blundering amanuensis, it has been corrected by Woodrow himself, and forms a part of the voluminous collection of MSS. made by that reverend minister as materials for his 'Account of the Sufferings of the Scottish Church'; and for another work which, from several papers in his library, he seems to have projected, but most unfortunately did not bring to perfection—'A History or Collection of Authentic Narratives respecting the Apparitions and Witchcraft of his Native Country.'" The author, Rev. Robert Law, was minister of Easter Kilpatrick, in the county of Dumbarton.

As the principal feature in Law's "Memorialls" consists in narratives of the doings of witchcraft and other matters partaking of the marvellous, Mr. Sharpe, in editing the work, very happily thought that an introduction tracing our legends of wizardry and spectral appearances to the earliest periods of Scottish history would be an appropriate addition to the work. This introduction amounts to nearly as much matter as that of the work to which it was prefixed, and is now regarded as probably the most important part of the volume. It is the best chronological and historical account of such matters in Scotland, and being strictly a monograph, quite independent of the "Memorialls" in every respect, it has been thought that it might very appropriately be printed by itself, and thus put within the reach of all; more especially as the original is a large quarto volume, now very scarce, and commanding a high price, debarring its possession from all but the few.

The present volume is that introduction, and is issued as sent out by Mr. Sharpe, only in some particulars the arrangement is slightly altered. In the original the page was a large quarto, permitting in several instances of extensive footnotes. These, as unsuitable for the present size of page, and as detracting from the continuity of the narrative, have, when it could be done with perfect propriety, been inserted in the body of the work. In instances where this could not be done properly, the notes have been transferred to the Appendix. Likewise in the present issue, the book is divided into chapters—a list of books on witchcraft in Scotland and an Index having been added. These additions the Editor hopes will enhance the value of the work, and render it still more interesting and attractive.

CONTENTS.

EDITORIAL NOTE, - - - - - - - - PAGE 5

BIOGRAPHICAL SKETCH OF THE AUTHOR, - - - - 11

CHAPTER I.

TO A.D. 1465.

In the days of King Caratake and Galgacus—The celebrated Witch of Iona—The Witches' Attack on St. Patrick—Wonderful Visions in the Year 697 A.D.—King Duffus and the Hags—Macbeth and the Three Weird Sisters—Thomas the Rhymer—The Enchanted Pear of Coalston—Wallace and the Apparition—Sir Michael Scott—Lord Soulis—The Red Cumyn—King James First and the Witch's Prophecy, - - - 17-32

CHAPTER II.

A.D. 1466 TO A.D. 1590.

Bishop Cameron—Earl of Mar—The Incubi and Succubi—A Young Man Bewitched—The Monster and the Gentlewoman—The Apparition and James IV.—The Execution of Lady Glammis—James V. and the Apparition—Queen Mary and Darnley—The Countess of Athole—The Family of Mark-Knox esteemed a Wizard—The Earl of Huntly—Lady Foullis and the Clay Pictures—Trial of Bessy Row, 33-54

CHAPTER III.

A.D. 1591 TO A.D. 1593.

The Famous Doctor Fian and his Associates—Their Doings and Trial—Doctor Fian's Confession—His Escape and Recapture —Put to the Torture—Burned on the Castle Hill, - 55-81

CHAPTER IV.

A.D. 1594 TO A.D. 1629.

The Earl of Argyle's Witch—The Countess of Arran deceived— Alison Balfour the Orkney Witch—James VI. and his "Dœmonologie"—The Earl of Gowrie and the Enchanted Parchment— The Murder of Kincaid—The Devil at Corstorphine—Lawrie Burned on the Castle Hill—The Burning of Isobel Grierson and Barbara Paterson—Curing and Inflicting Diseases,
82-100

CHAPTER V.

A.D. 1630 TO A.D. 1644.

Drummond of Auchterarder—Catherine Oswald's Indictment— Tested by the Insertion of a Pin—Hattaraick Burned on the Castle Hill—The Indictment against Alie Nisbet—James Spalding Buried Alive—Many Witches on the Coasts of Fife —A notorious Warlock Worried at the Stake—Executions of Barker and Lauder—The Indictment against Agnes Fynnie,
101-119

CHAPTER VI.

A.D. 1645 TO A.D. 1669.

The Death of Charles I. and Civil War Predicted—Hidden Treasure supposed to be guarded by Spirits—Davy Ramsay, Clockmaker—The Marquis of Montrose influenced—Strange Sights at General Leshley's House—Precognition of Approaching Death—The Earl of Holland's Death—Two "Remarkables" —Numerous Witch Burnings on the Restoration of Charles II. —The Cases of Margaret Bryson, Isabel Ramsay, and Margaret Hutcheson, - - - - - - - 119-143

CHAPTER VII.

A.D. 1668 TO A.D. 1683.

Strange Apparitions in the Covenanting Times—At Rutherglen—At Craigmad—At Darmead—Curious Beliefs regarding the Royalists on the part of the Covenanters—The Ghost of Spedlins Castle—"The Laying of a Gaist"—Wonderful Revelations at Monzie—A Witch Burned at Crieff—Graves Unaccountably Prepared, - - - - - 143-160

CHAPTER VIII.

A.D. 1684 TO A.D. 1718.

Witchcraft in Dumfriesshire—Jonet Fraser's Remarkable Revelations—Additional Incidents in 1687—The Rev. T. Forrester's Dream—Showers of Hats, Guns, and Swords near Lanark—The Viscount Dundee's Ghost—The Renfrewshire Witches—The Pittenweem Witches—Spirits Troubling the House of the Minister of Kinross, - - - - - - 160-180

CHAPTER IX.

A.D. 1718 TO A.D. 1719.

Curious Account of a Case of Witchcraft in Caithness—James Fraser's Letter to Woodrow—The Lord-Advocate's Letter to the Sheriff-Depute, Caithness—The Sheriff's Answer—William Montgomerie's Petition—Margaret Nin-Gilbert's Examination and Confession, - - - - - - - 180-194

CHAPTER X.

A.D. 1720 TO A.D. 1724.

Lord Torphichen's Son Bewitched—The Tinklerian Doctor—The last Execution of a Scottish Witch—The Statutes regarding Witchcraft Repealed—The Elgin Wonder—The Minister of Salcraig—Rutherford's Revelations—The Laird of Cool's Ghost, - - - - - - - - 194-206

APPENDIX.

The Conveyance of Individuals through the Air by Witchcraft,	207
The Marks of a Witch,	208
Sickness laid beneath a Barn Door,	210
On Burying and Burning Animals Alive,	210
Peculiar Caps of the Seventeenth Century,	212
Lord Holland's Daughters,	213
On Devilish Charms,	216
Familiar Spirits,	217
Females in Masculine Attire,	218
The Duke of Lauderdale on Witchcraft,	219
Singular and Laughable Account of the Doings of a Spirit in Kirkcudbrightshire,	229

EDITORIAL APPENDIX.

Short List of Books on Scottish Witchcraft and Superstition,	255
INDEX,	263

BIOGRAPHICAL SKETCH OF THE AUTHOR.

CHARLES KIRKPATRICK SHARPE, the highly-gifted author of the following work, and well-known in the literary circles of Edinburgh during the first half of the present century, was born at Hoddam Castle, Annandale, on the 15th May, 1781, the third son of Charles Sharpe of Hoddam.

His father, Charles Sharpe, was grandson of Sir Thomas Kirkpatrick of Closeburn, who again on his mother's side was descended from the Earls of Mar and the Dukes of Lennox. This illustrious descent on his father's side was highly interesting to our author, Mr. Sharpe. Hardly less did he value his descent through his grandmother, Lady Susan Renton, from the Eglinton family. His immediate ancestress, the beautiful Countess Susannah, was a favourite subject of his pencil and pen. His eldest brother was the late General Sharpe of Hoddam, who long represented the Dumfries Burghs in Parliament.

Being a younger son, he was educated with a view probably of entering one of the professions, which intention, however, if there was any such, was never given effect to.

Having attended the College classes at Edinburgh University, Mr. Sharpe matriculated at Christ Church, Oxford, in November, 1798, where he graduated as B.A. in 1802, and M.A. in 1806. The death of his father in 1813, and the settlement of his mother in Edinburgh, induced him after that date to fix his permanent residence in that city, which he accordingly did, and settled himself in the position which he kept to the last, namely, that of a man of fashion, devoting his life to the pleasures of society, and to the successful cultivation of literature, music, and the fine arts. He likewise gave a large amount of attention to objects of antiquarian and artistic interest, forming an immense collection of books, manuscripts, china, paintings, engravings, musical instruments, and other articles of *vertu* or curiosity. This collection, it is supposed, was probably the most unique ever accumulated by a private individual in Scotland.

In manners Mr. Sharpe was polished and aristocratic, somewhat capricious and eccentric, but at the same time extremely affable and obliging, and ever ready to give information regarding literary and antiquarian matters, as likewise to show his collection to interested friends. He has been termed the Sir Horace Walpole of Edinburgh. Throughout life Mr. Sharpe formed a very large circle of acquaintances, persons mostly of considerable social or literary note, and carried on a most voluminous correspondence. Foremost among his friends at Oxford appear the names of the Duke of Sutherland, the Earl of Lanesborough, Stapleton (son of Lord le De Spencer), Conybeare (Professor of poetry in 1812), Inglis (who subsequently represented the University in Parliament), Sir James Macdonald, the Earls of Beauchamp, Granville, Somerset, and many others whose names occur in the course of his correspondence. Foremost among his Edinburgh friends may be mentioned Thosas Thomson, David Laing, and Sir Walter Scott.

Of an active disposition both in mind and body, Mr. Sharpe's pen was constantly in use writing articles of various descriptions and editing manuscripts for the press. Foremost among his literary labours may be mentioned the following:—The *Ballad Book*, a small collection of Scottish ballads inscribed to Sir Walter Scott; Law's *Memorialls*, edited from manuscript, a work repeatedly referred to by historical writers as a book of authority, and of which the most important part is probably the voluminous introduction, purely from the pen of the editor. He likewise edited with large notes Kirkton's *History of the Church of Scotland*, and superintended the printing of Sir R. Maitland's *History of the House of Seytoun* for the Bannatyne Club. In addition to the foregoing a considerable number of smaller publications came through his hands —the *Life of Lady Margaret Cunningham; A Memorial of the Conversion of Jean Livingston; Letters of Lady Margaret Kennedy; Letters of Archibald Earl of Argyle; Minuets and Songs* by Thomas, sixth Earl of Kelly; *Sargundo*, or the Valiant Christian. All the foregoing, as also anything else that may have come from the pen of our author, are exceedingly scarce, and only to be found in the hands of a few collectors. In each instance the number of copies printed was exceedingly limited.

Distinguished as an antiquarian and poet, Mr. Sharpe gave proof of a still higher skill in the fine arts, many of his copper etchings and original drawings attaining quite an extensive celebrity. The productions were very numerous. Among many others may be mentioned " Queen Elizabeth Dancing High and Disposedly " before the Scottish Envoy, Sir James Melville; the "Marriage of Mucklemou'd Meg," illustrating a well-known incident in Border history; the " Battle of Bothwell Bridge," from a picture at Dalkeith house; portraits of the Duke and Duchess of Lauderdale, from pictures by Lely; " the Witch of Fyfe," a character from one of the tales of " The Queen's Wake," by Hogg; "A Lady with her Flirt and a Fool," a frontispiece to the *Ballad Book;* "The Owl kneeling to the Peacock," a frontispiece to *The Howlet;* "The Lady and the Knight," a frontispiece to the romance of *Sir Greysteel;* "The Lover's Message," a frontispiece to lines by the Earl of Kelly. In addition to these there are many others.

On the death of his brother in 1841, Mr. Sharpe

succeeded to the family inheritance of Hoddam. He continued, however, to reside chiefly in Edinburgh, and enjoyed himself in the indulgence of his favourite pursuits. He died unmarried on the 17th March, 1851, at his own residence in Drummond Place, Edinburgh, and was buried with his forefathers in the family mausoleum at Hoddam. Since his decease a new and enlarged edition of the *Ballad Book* has been issued. There likewise appeared in 1869 a large and most interesting volume containing his etchings, original drawings, political and prose fragments, and a memoir. Interspersed throughout the memoir are numerous extracts from his correspondence, which are exceedingly characteristic, and forcibly portray the man and his tastes.

A HISTORICAL ACCOUNT

OF THE BELIEF IN

WITCHCRAFT IN SCOTLAND.

CHAPTER I.

TO A.D. 1465.

In the days of King Caratake and Galgacus—The celebrated Witch of Iona—The Witches' Attack on St. Patrick— Wonderful Visions in the Year 697 A.D.—*King Duffus and the Hags—Macbeth and the Three Weird Sisters— Thomas the Rhymer—The Enchanted Pear of Coalston — Wallace and the Apparition—Sir Michael Scott— Lord Soulis—The Red Cumyn—King James First and the Witch's Prophecy.*

THE first *strange sights*, as Mr. Raphael Hollinshed terms them, which we meet with in Scottish Chronicles, occur in the reign of King Caratake, himself the eighteenth of Caledonia's visionary monarchs; apparitions of horsemen fighting and slaying each other—wolves which carried off to the woods a shepherd keeping his flock by night, and suffered him to escape again. "Moreover, in Carrick was a child born, perfect in all his limbs, saving the head, which was like unto a raven's."

It should have been an eagle's; for these wonders were all portentous of Caratake's battles with the Romans, his Italian captivity, and subsequent return to Scotland.

Thus also, when Corbreid Gald, or Galgacus, marched against the squadrons of Italy, and sustained a signal defeat, "an eagle was seene almost a whole day, fleeing up and downe over the Scotish armie, even as though she had laboured herself wearie; also an armed man was seen flieing about the armie, and suddenlie vanished away. There fell, in like manner, out of a dark cloud in the fields, through the which the armie should pass, divers kinds of birds that were spotted with blood." King Mogall was suspected to have known through witchcraft of that conspiracy against him to which he fell a victim in the year 169. In the reign of Natholocus, a witch dwelt in Iona, so celebrated for her skill, that the king, when compelled to withdraw from the attacks of his rebellious subjects, sent one of his trusty followers to consult her as to the issue of the war. "The witch, consulting with her spirits, declared in the end, how it should come shortlie to pass that the king should be murdered, not by his open enemies, but by the hands of one of his most familiar friends, in whom he had reposed an especiall trust. The messenger demanded by whose hands that should be? 'Even by thine,' said she, 'as shall be well known within these few dayes.' The gentleman, hearing these words, railed against her verie bitterlie, bidding her go like an old witch, for he trusted to see her burnt before he should commit so villanous a deed. And, departing from her, he went by and by to signifie what answer he had received; but before he came where the king lay, his mind was altered, so that, what for doubt on the one side, that if he should declare the truth as it was told him, the king might, happlie, conceive some great suspicion that it should follow by his meanes as she had declared, and thereupon put him to death first; and for feare, on the other side, that if he keepe it secret, it might happen to be revealed by some other, and then he to run in as much danger of life as before. He determined with himself to work the surest way, and so coming to the king, he was led aside by him into his privie chamber, when all other being commanded to avoid, he declared how he had sped; and then falling forthwith upon Natholocus with a dagger, he slew him outright."

About the year 388, the singular piety of St. Patrick, according to tradition, became so offensive to the devil, that he incensed the whole body of witches in Scotland against him. In a band they assailed the astonished saint, who fled towards the river Clyde, near the mouth of which he found a little boat, wherein he immediately leapt, and set off for Ireland. It is well known that witches cannot cross a running stream in pursuit of their prey; but these tore a huge fragment of rock from a neighbouring hill and hurled it after Patrick, taking, however, so bad an aim, that the mass fell harmless to the ground, and afterwards, with some additions from art, became the fortress of Dumbarton.

An. Do. 697, many *wonderful visions* were seen in Scotland. In the remoter parts it rained blood; and in the church of Camelon there was heard a noise, as if it had been the clattering of armour. In the same city, before its destruction by Kenneth, "as the bishop was at service, holding his crocier staffe in his hand,' it was kindled so with fire, that by no meane it could be quenched, till it was burnt even to ashes. About noone-daie, the aire being faire and cleare, as well in the countries of the Scots as of the Picts, there was heard such a noise and clattering of weapons and armor, with braieng of horses, as though two armies should have beene together in fight, whereby manie of either nation who heard it were put in great feare."—Hollinshed. N.B.—The said King Kenneth, among the laws attributed to him, ordained that jugglers, wizards, necromancers, and such as call up spirits, "and use to seek upon them for helpe, let them be burnt to death."

King Duffus's danger from witchcraft is detailed by Buchanan and other historians, and by Law himself, page 112. A company of hags roasted his image made of wax upon a wooden spit, reciting certain words of enchantment, and basting the figure with a poisonous liquor. These women, when apprehended, declared, that as the wax melted, the body of the king should decay, and the words of enchantment prevented him from the refreshment of sleep.

"His picture made in wax, and gently molten
By a blue fire, kindled with dead men's eyes,
Will waste him by degrees."
—Middleton's *Witch*.

Duffus recovered his health after the destruction of the image; and the witches were burnt at Forres in Murray. The murder of this king, continue our Chronicle writers, occasioned many wonders. Horses in Lothian, remarkable for swiftness and beauty, devoured their own flesh, nor would they taste any other food. In Angus, a gentlewoman brought forth a child without eyes, nose, hands, or feet; a sparrowhawk was strangled by an owl; and the sun was completely veiled in clouds for the tedious space of six months.

Macbeth's adventure with the three weird sisters is the next remarkable event in our miraculous annals. They were dressed in strange and wild apparel, like people of *the elder world;* and it appears doubtful, whether they were mortal witches, or nymphs, *alias* fairies, who are supposed to be always on good terms with the others, whom they resemble in their evil propensities. In the *Recueil de Dissertations sur les Apparitions,* &c., printed at Avignon, 1751, is a story of a cup seized by a countryman at a banquet of these fairies, and presented to King Henry the First of England. It was of an extraordinary composition and colour, bearing no resemblance to common cups. Henry sent it to the king of Scotland, and it was preserved with great care in the royal treasury, till William the Lion restored it to England as a gift to Henry the Second. The drinking-glass at Eden-Hall, in Cumberland, is consecrated by a similar legend.

Cleland, in his *Effigies Clericorum,* attributes the disappearance of the Scottish fairies to the Reformation. Talking of Parnassus, he observes—

"There's als much virtue, sense, and pith,
In Annan, or the Water of Nith,
Which quietly slips by Dumfries,
Als any water in all Greece.
For there, and several other places,
About mill-dams, and green brae faces,
Both Elrich elfs and brownies stayed,

And green-gown'd fairies daunc'd and played:
When old John Knox, and other some,
Began to plott the Haggs of Rome;
Then suddenly took to their heels,
And did no more frequent these fields;
But if Rome's pipes perhaps they hear,
Sure, for their interest they'll compear
Again, and play their old hell's tricks," &c.

In the year 1285, during the nuptial festivities of Alexander the Third at Jedburgh, a ghost, or something resembling a ghost, danced at a ball. Fordun says,—" Insecutus est unus, de quo pene dubitari potuit utrum homo esset an phantasma; qui ut umbra magis labi videbatur, quam pedetentim transire." And Boece positively affirms that it was a skeleton.—" Effigies hominis mortui, carne nudatis ejus ossibus, visa est."

In the reign of the same monarch flourished that mysterious prophet, wizard, semi-mortal, and poet, Thomas of Ercildoun, commonly called the Rymer, whose romance of Sir Tristrem has been of late so ably edited by Mr. Scott, after giving the world some previous notices of true Thomas, in the second volume of the Border Minstrelsy; to those the reader is referred for many interesting particulars respecting the Nostradamus of Scotland, as well as of the Caledonian Merlin, with whose prophecies and adventures those of the other have been frequently blended and obscured. A contemporary of Thomas the Rymer was Hugh Gifford, Lord of Yester, esteemed a notable magician. He formed, by magic art, in his Castle of Yester, a capacious cavern, called Bohall, that is, Hobgoblin Hall,— (Fordun, ii. 105.)—a spacious room, with a vaulted roof, which still remains entire. It may be observed, that the heiress of his family married Sir William Hay of Locharret, ancestor of John, third Lord Hay of Yester, whose daughter, Jean, became the wife of Brown of Coalston. This lady's dowry consisted of a single pear, probably enchanted by her ancestor, Hugh Gifford, which her father declared to be invaluable; assuring the Laird of Coalston, that whilst the pear was preserved in the family, it would certainly continue to flourish. This palladium is still carefully treasured up; but there is a mark on one side, made by the eager teeth of a lady of Coalston, who, while breeding, longed for the forbidden fruit, and was permitted to take one bite by her too-indulgent husband; in consequence, some of the best farms on the estate very speedily came to market. Crawford, the peerage writer, thus mentions the superstition in his MS. Account of the Browns of Coalston:—"They had a pear in their family, which they esteemed yer palladium; it's reported, that Betty Mackenzie, when she married George Brown of Colstoun, the first night she came to the house of Colstoun, dreamed she had eat the pear, which her father-in-law looked on as a bad omen, and expressed great fears that she should be an instrument in the destruction of the house of Colstoun."

One of the most poetical passages in Blind Harry's Life of Wallace, contains an account of an apparition seen by the hero, after slaying Fawdoune, an Irishman of suspicious character, who accompanied him in his flight from the English forces at Black-erne Side. The enemy were aided in their pursuit by a blood-hound, whose course Wallace thus stopt—"While she gat blood, no fleeing might prevail,"—if he did not avenge himself of a treacherous friend's perfidy. He afterwards repaired to the Tower of Gask.

" Threteyn war left with hym, no mar had he,
  In the Gask hall yair lugying haiff yai tayne,
  Fyr gat yai sone, bot meyt yan had yai nane ;
  Twa scheipe yai tuk besyde yaim off a fauld,
  Ordanyt to soupe into yat sembly hauld ;
  Graithit in haist sum fude for yaim to dycht,
  So hard yai blaw rude hornss upon hycht.
  Twa sende he furth to luk quhat it myght be,
  Yai bad rycht lang, and no tithings hard he,
  Bot boustouss noyis so brymly blow and fast,

So oyir twa into ye wode furth past.
Nane come agayne bot boustously can blaw,
Into gret ire he send them furth on raw.
Quhen yat allayne Wallace was lewyt yar,
Ye awfull blast aboundyt mekill mar;
Yan trewit he weille yai had hys lugyng seyne,
Hys suerd he drew, of nobill mettall keyne,
Syne furth he went quhar at he hard ye horn,
Without ye dur Fawdoun was hym beforn,
As till hys sicht, hys awne hede in hys hand,
A croyss he maid quhen he saw hym so stand.
At Wallace in ye hede he swaket yar,
And he in haist sone hynt it by ye hair;
Syne out at hym agayne he couth it cast,
Intill hys hart he was gretlye agast.
Richt weill he trowit yat was na spreit of man
It was sum dewill, at sic malice began.
He wyst na weill yar langar for to byde,
Up throw ye hall yus wycht Wallace can glyde.
To a closs stayr, the burds raiff in twyne,
Fyftyne fute large he lap out of yat inn.
Up ye wattir sedeynlye he couth fair,
Agayne he blent quhat perance he saw yair,
He thocht he saw Fawdoune, yat ugly syr,
Yat haill hall he had sett in a fyr;
A gret raftre he had intill hys hand,
Wallace as yan no langar wold he stand," &c.

Wallace, b. 5.

This period of Scottish history is remarkable for two very celebrated enchanters, Lord Soulis, and Sir Michael Scott of Balweary. Sir Michael was a man of considerable learning, and, if tradition is to be believed, a great benefactor to his country—with the aid of the devil, indeed, who now and then condescended, for purposes best known to himself, to help Sir Michael in his philanthropic undertakings, such as forming the road through Locher-Moss, in Dumfries-shire, which these friends are supposed to have completed in the short space of one night. For many particulars concerning *Auld Michael of Baldwearie*, see The Lay of the Last Minstrel, Notes to The Mountain Bard, and the excellent poem of Anster Fair.

Sir Michael Scott is said to have been buried either at Home-Cultram, in Cumberland, or Melrose Abbey; but his tomb is now fixed at the latter by the great poetical magician of his own name, who adds,—

> " Within it burns a wonderous light,
> To chase the spirits that love the night:
> That lamp shall burn unquenchably,
> Until the eternal doom shall be."

See the note to these verses for some curious circumstances respecting such lamps. Baptista

Porta mentions a most extraordinary and dangerously-devised lamp, well known, it would appear, in his time, whose properties were quite as wonderful as the immortality of the sepulchral lights. "To let nothing pass that jugglers and impostors counterfeit, they set a lamp, with characters graved upon it, and filled with hare's fat; then they mumble forth some words, and light it; when it burns in the middle of women's company, it constrains them all to cast off their clothes, and the women will never leave dancing so long as the lamp burns; and this was related to me by men of credit. I believe this effect can come from nothing but the hare's fat, the force whereof, perhaps, is venemous, and penetrating the brain, moves them to this madness." Quere, Do not the villanous oil-merchants of the present day light up our ball-rooms with something of the same nature? See also Reginald Scott's Discovery of Witchcraft, b. 13. c. 30.

William Lord Soulis was a wizard of a much more pernicious description. The Castle of Hermitage, the scene of his foul sorceries, and every species of wickedness, is said to have sunk partially into the earth, unable to bear the load of those accumulated crimes; and he himself, with appropriate cruelty, was boiled to death in a cauldron, at a place called the Nine-Stane Rig, by persons whom the king had unwarily

authorised to execute so barbarous a sentence.—
Border Minstrelsy, vol. ii.

In the year 1306, Robert Bruce stabbed John Cumyn, regent of Scotland, in the Dominical church of Dumfries; and the daggers of Roger Kirkpatrick of Closeburne, and of James Lindsay, completed the murder. Bowmaker informs us, that the corpse of the regent was afterwards watched by the Dominicans, with the usual ceremonies of the church. At the middle hour of the night, the whole assistants fell into the most profound slumber, saving one aged father, who heard with terror and astonishment, a voice, like that of a wailing infant, exclaim,—" How long, O Lord, shall vengeance be deferred?" It was answered in a dreadful tone,—"Endure with patience until the anniversary of this day shall return for the fifty-second time." In the year 1357, fifty-two years after the Red Cumyn's death, Sir James Lindsay was hospitably feasted in the Castle of Caerlaveroc, in Dumfries-shire, belonging to Roger Kirkpatrick. They were the sons of the regent's murderers. At midnight, for some cause unknown, Lindsay arose, and with a poniard assassinated his sleeping host. He then mounted his horse and fled; but after riding all night, he was taken at day-break, not three miles from the Castle, and executed for his crime at Dumfries.—*Vide* Wintowne's *Cronykill*, b. 8.

cap. 44; *Border Minstrelsy*, vol. iii. p. 328. This apprehension of Sir James Lindsay, so near the spot where he had committed the murder, resembles that of Poltrot de Meré, the assassin of the Duke of Guise, who, after riding the whole night among the woods, was seized in the morning near the bridge of Olivet, only one league from Orleans.

From the contemporary account of the barbarous murder of King James the First, at Perth, in the year 1437, printed by Mr. Pinkerton, we learn that the monarch's fate was predicted by an Irish prophetess, or witch.—" The kyng, sodanly avised, made a solempne fest of the Christynmes at Perth, which is clepid Sant John's Town, which is from Edenbourgh on that other side of the Scottish see, the which is vulgarly clepid the Water of Lethe. Yn the myddis of the way, thare arose a woman of Yreland, that clepid herselfe as a suthsayer. The which anone as she saw the kyng, she cried with lowde voise, saying thus :—' My lord kyng, and ye pase this water, ye shall never turne agane on lyve.' The kyng heryng this, was astonyed of her wordis; for bot a litile to fore he had red in a prophesie, that yn the selfe same yere the kyng of Scottes shuld be slayne; and therwithall the kyng, as he rode, clepid to him one of his knyghtis, and gave hym in commandment to torne agane to speke

with that woman, and ask of here what sheo wold,
and what thyng sheo ment with her lowd crying?
And sheo began, and told hym as ye hafe hard of
the kynge of Scottes yf he passed that water.
As now the kynge askid her, how sheo knew
that? And sheo said, that Huthart told her so.
'Sire,' quod ho, 'men may calant ye tak non hede
of yond woman's wordes, for sheo nys bot a
drunkine fule, and wot not what sheo saith;' and
so, with his folk, passid the water clepid the
Scottishe see, towards Saynt Johnnes Towne."
The narrator states some dreams ominous of
James's murder, and afterwards proceeds thus:
—"Both afore soper, and long aftir ynto quarter
of the nyght, in the which the Erle of Athetelles,
and Robert Stward were aboute the kyng, where
thay wer occupied att the playng of the chesse,
att the tables, yn redying of romans, yn syngyng
and pyping, yn harping, and in other honest
solaces of grete pleasance and disport. Therwith
came the said woman of Yreland, that clepid herself a dyvenourese, and entered the kynge's courte,
till that sheo came streght to the kynge's chambur-
dore, where sheo stood, and abode bycause that
hit was shitte. And fast sheo knokyd, till at the
last the usher opyned the dure, marvelyng of that
woman's beyng there that tyme of the nyght, and
askyng here what sheo wold? 'Let me yn, sire,'
quod sheo, 'for I haf sumwhat to say, and to tell

unto the kyng; for I am the same woman that noght long agone desired to haf spokyn with hym at the Lith, whan he should passe the Scottish see.' The usher went yn and told hym of this woman. 'Yea,' quod the kyng, 'let hir cume tomorrow;' bycause that he was occupied with suche disportes at that tyme, hym let not to entend her as thenne. The usher came agane to the chamber-dore, to the said woman, and there he told hir that the kyng was besye in playing, and bid her cum soon agane upon the morrow. 'Well,' said the woman, 'hit shall repent yow all that ye wil not let me speke nowe with the kyng.' Therat the usher lughe, and held her bot a fule, chargyng her to go her way, and therwithall she went thens." The Earl of Athole, one of the chief conspirators, was afterwards, at his execution, crowned with a regal diadem of red-hot iron, because, says Buchanan, certain witches, for whom the county of Athole was always infamous, had told him that he would be crowned a king in sight of all the people. The historian sagely adds,—" Idque vaticinium ita vel impletum vel elusum est: ac certe tales predictiones frequenter hujusmodi sortiuntur eventus."

CHAPTER II.

A.D. 1466 TO A.D. 1590.

Bishop Cameron—Earl of Mar—The Incubi and Succubi—A Young Man Bewitched—The Monster and the Gentlewoman—The Apparition and James IV.—The Execution of Lady Glammis—James V. and the Apparition—Queen Mary and Darnley—The Countess of Athole—The Family of Mark—Knox esteemed a Wizard—The Earl of Huntly—Lady Fowllis and the Clay Pictures--Trial of Bessy Row.

IN the year 1466, the night before Christmas-day, as John Cameron, Bishop of Glasgow, a man of a wicked life, lay asleep in his house of Lockwood, a loud clap of thunder roused him, followed immediately by a voice, charging him to appear before the tribunal of God, to be tried for his manifold crimes. The startled prelate called for his attendants and lights, and sitting up upon his bed, began to read a book, when a second clap of thunder, and the same words, were heard by all; a third time the thunder and the summons were repeated, but in a still louder manner, when the bishop fell back upon the bed, and expired with one heavy groan, his tongue hanging out of his mouth as if he had died from strangulation.—(Buchanan, Pitscottie.)

The disastrous fate of the Earl of Mar in the

year 1479 was, in some measure, occasioned by an accusation of practising magic, which he was alleged to have directed against the king his brother's life. Several authors impute the enmity of James against Mar and Albany to a prophecy of some witches, to whom, says Buchanan, the monarch was greatly addicted, or of Andrew, a Flemish astrologer, favoured by the king, who affirmed, that in Scotland a lion should be devoured by his whelps. Twelve mean women, and several wizards, accused of having employed diabolic arts in the service of Mar, by roasting the king in a waxen effigy, were burnt at Edinburgh soon after the murder of that unhappy prince.

About the year 1480, if we may yield credit to Boece, the wicked spirits Incubi and Succubi (for a curious account of which see Scott's Discovery of Witchcraft) were exceedingly troublesome in Scotland. A ship sailing out of the Forth towards Flanders, in the middle of summer, was assailed with a furious tempest, which increased with such vehemence that the mariners, astonished at so singular a hurricane, during the mildest season of the year, gave themselves up for lost; when a woman, who had taken refuge below, called to them to throw her overboard into the sea, as the only means of preserving their own lives, confessing that she had been long haunted with an Incubus, wearing the likeness of a man, in whose embraces she was at that very moment speaking. Luckily for all parties, there chanced to be a priest in the ship, who hastened to the poor woman's rescue; and after a long admonition, followed by many sighs and tears of the wretched penitent, "there issued forth of the pumpe of the ship," says Hollinshed, " a foul and evil favoured blacke cloud, with a mightie terrible noise, flame, smoke, and stinke, which presentlie fell into the sea, and suddenlie thereupon the tempest ceassed, and the ship passing in great quiet the residue of her journie, arrived in safetie at the place whither she was bound."

Not long before this event, a young man, near Aberdeen, remarkable for his personal attractions, complained to the bishop of the diocese that he was infested by a spirit in the shape of a female, "so fair and beautiful a thing that he never saw the like," which would come to his chamber at night and endeavour to allure him to her embraces. The bishop wisely advised him to remove into another country, and addict himself to fasting and prayer, which measure had the desired effect; a thing wonderful enough, considering the wicked perseverance of these spirits, as distinguished for their unwearied pursuit of their victims (vide Cazotte's *Diable Amoureux*), as for their subsequent constancy. Benoit, a wizard of Berne, was burnt alive at the age of 75, after confessing, that for *forty years* he had kept up an amatory commerce with a Succubus, called Hermeline; and Mirandula mentions one Pinet, a man aged 80, convicted of a like protracted commerce with a spirit named Florina.

"About the same time also," continues Hollinshed from Boethius, " there was in the countrie of Mar a young gentlewoman of excellent beautie, and daughter unto a nobleman there, refusing sundrie wealthie mariages offered to her by her father, and other friends. At length she prooved with child, and being rigorouslie compelled by her parents to tell who was the father, she confessed that a certain young man used nightly to come unto her, and kept her companie, and sometimes in the day also, but how or from whence he came, or by what meanes he went awaie, she was not able to declare. Her parents, not greatlie crediting her words, laid diligent watch, to understand what he was that had defiled their house; and within three days after, upon signification given by one of their maidens, that the fornicator was at that very instant with their daughter, incontinentlie thereupon, making fast the doors, they enter the chamber with a great manie of torches and lights, where they find in their daughter's armes a foul monstrous thing, verie horrible to behold. Here a number coming hastilie in, to behold this evil favoured sight, amongst others, there was a priest of verie honest life, not ignorant (as was thought) in knowledge of holie scripture. This priest (all other being afraid), and some of them running their waies, began to recite the beginning of St. John's Gospell, and coming to these words, *Verbum caro factum est*, suddenlie the wicked spirit, making a very sore and terrible roaring noise, flue his waies, taking the roofe of the chamber away with him, the hangings and coverings of the bed being also burnt therewith. The gentlewoman was yet preserved, and within three or four daies after was delivered of such a mishapen thing, as the like before had not beene seene, which the midwives and women, such as were present at her labour, to avoid the dishonour of her house, immediately burnt in a great fire, made in the chamber for the same intent."—(See Du Rosset's *Histoires Tragiques*, for a dismal story of a young lady beloved by a spirit.) But the most curious incident of this nature which I have met with is quoted by Richard Baxter from Scribonius. "Near Witeberg, a merchant's wife that passed for an honest woman, was used to admit one peculiar concubine; and once, her husband being from home, her lover came to her in the night, and having pleased his love, in the morning he arose, and sate on the top of the door in the shape of a magpye, and said to her this farewell,—' *Hitherto this hath been thy sweet-heart,*' and vanished with the words."—*Certainty of the World of Spirits,* p. 102. " I rather think that this was a man-witch than a devil," adds Baxter, but for what reason, unluckily, he does not say.

For an account of the apparition which admonished James the Fourth previous to the battle of Flodden, and of the voice heard in the silence of night at the Cross of Edinburgh, summoning the devoted host to the tribunal of Plotcock, the reader is referred to the Notes on Marmion; but much less dignified prodigies announced the issue of that fatal conflict. In the council of war, held by James to arrange the order of battle, a hare appeared, and escaped through a thousand arrows, daggers, and other things, aimed at her by the shouting assembly. The same night mice gnawed asunder the leather-strap of James's helmet, by which it was usually suspended from the tester of his bed; and at day-break, a dewy moisture, resembling blood, appeared to stain the inner curtains of the royal tent.

The annals of James the Fifth's reign are disgraced with the execution of Lady Janet Douglas, sister of the Earl of Angus, widow of John Lyon Lord Glammis, and wife of Archibald Campbell of Kepneith. She was accused, together with her husband, her son the Lord

Glammis, John Lyon his relation, and an old priest, of having meditated the death of James, by poison or witchcraft, with the intention of restoring the house of Angus. The following extract respecting her trial is taken from an abridgement of the Criminal Records of Edinburgh. " July 17, 1537.—Janeta Douglas, Domina de Glammis, convicted by the assize, viz. Earl of Athole, Earl of Buchan, Lord Maxwell, Master of Glencairne, Home of Coldinknows, Kirkpatrick of Kirkmichael, Crichton of Ravennis, Ker of Mersington, Earl of Cassillis, Lord Semple, Laird of Raith, Tower of Inverleith, Barclay of Mathers, Edmonston of that ilk, M'Lellan, tutor of Bomby. *Sententia Forisfacturæ.* It is fundin be the said assize, that Janet Douglas, Lady of Glamis, hes committed art and part of the treasonable consperation and magination of the slaughter and destruction of our sovereign Lord his most noble person by poyson, and for art and part of the treasonable assistance, supply, intercommuning, and fortifying of Archibald, sometime Earl of Angus, and George Douglas his brother, rebells and traitors, in a treasonable manner. For the whilk treasonable crimes the said Janet, Lady of Glamis, be forfaulted to our sovereign Lord, her life, lands, goods, moveable and immoveable, and that she shall be had to the Castle-hill of Edinburgh, and there burnt in ane fire to the dead as ane traitor; and that I gif for doom."—From dates, it appears that this noble witch, who was as remarkable for her beauty and courage, as for her dismal fate, was hurried from the bar to the stake, where she died with great composure, amid the loud lamentations of the multitude.

In Dunbar's poem, called The Dream of the Abbot of Tungland, (an Italian mountebank, who composed a pair of wings, and attempted to fly to France from the walls of Stirling Castle, 1503-7) mention is made of a witch, concerning whose biography the editor is completely in the dark :—

" Undir Saturnus fyrie regioun,
Symone Magus sall meit him, and Mahoun;
And Merlyne at the mone sall hym be bydand,
And *Jonet the widow* on ane besome rydand,
Of wichis with an windrous garesoun."

King James the Fifth was reported to have seen in dreams, a short time previous to his death, the apparitions of two persons, who were supposed to have lost their souls in his service. Of this, Knox gives the following account:— " Yit did not God ceiss to gif that blindit prince some documentis that some suddane plague was to fall upoun him, in caiss he did not repent his wicked lyif, and that his awin mouthe did confesse; for after that Sir James Hamiltoun was behided (justlie or injustlie, we dispute not) this visioun cam unto him, as to his familiaris himsalf did declair; the said Sir James apeired unto him, havand in his hand ane drawn sword, be the quhilk fra the king he straik bayth the airmes, saying to him thir wordis, 'Tak that, quhill thou resave a finall payment for all thine impitie.' This visioun, with sorrowful continance, he schew one the morne, and schortlie thairefter deid his two sonis, both within the spaice of 24 hours; yea, some say, within the spaice of sex hours. How terribil a visioun the said prince saw, lying in Linlithgow, that nycht Thomas Scott, Justice-Clerk, died in Edinburgh, men of gude credite can yit reporte; for affrayit at midnycht or efter, he cryit for torches, and raissit all that lay besyde him in the pallace, and tould that Tome Scot was deid; for he had bein at him with a cumpayne of devillis, and had said unto him this word, 'O wo to the day that evir I knew thee or thy service; for, for serving of the, against God, against his servants, and against justice, I ame adjugit to endles torment.' "—Knox's *History*, p. 24.

The reign of James's unhappy daughter, as it abounded in other crimes, so it was fruitful of witchcraft. The Lady Buccleuch, whom Mr. Scott has immortalized in the Lay of the Last Minstrel, belonging to a family distinguished for talent, and endowed with a masculine courage,

was said to have gained the queen's consent to the murder of Darnley through her witchcraft,—backed by the persuasions of Bothwell, indeed, which, was Marie really conscious of the plot, may be justly suspected the stronger stimulus of the twain. Buchanan thus notices two *ostenta*, which preceded the murder of Darnley:—
" Jacobus Londinus, homo Fifanus, honesto loco natus, cum febri diu laborasset, pridie quam Rex occideretur, circa meridiem, in lecto se paullum erexit, ac, velut attonitus, magna voce obtestatus est præsentes ; 'Ut Regi opem ferrent: jam enim parricidas eum invadere.' Deinde, paullo post, cum flebili questu exclamavit ; 'Frustra opem feretis ; jam trucidatus est.' Nec ipse diu post eam vocem supervixit. Alterum cum cœde ipsa conjunctum fuit. Tres e familiaribus comitis Atholiæ, Regis propinqui, homines et virtute et genere minime obscuri, non procul a Regis hospitio divertebant : iis circiter mediam noctem dormientibus, ad Dugallum Stuartum, qui proxime parietem accubabat, quidam visus est accedere, ac manu leviter per barbam malamque ducta, eum excitare, dicens ; 'Surgite, vim vobis afferunt.' Is experrectus repente, cum visum secum revolveret, alius confestim ex alio lecto exclamat ; ' Quis me calcat ? ' Et cum Dugallus respondisset : ' Felem esse fortasse, qui (ut fit) noctu oberraret :' tum tertius, qui nondum experrectus

fuerat, statim e lecto se conjecit in pedes, rogitans; 'Quis colaphum sibi incussisset:' et cum dicto, per ostium visus est quispiam egredi, nec sine strepitu. Interea, dum illi visa et audita inter se conferunt, domus Regiæ cadentis fragor auditus omnes consternavit."

The Countess of Athole, too, was another lady much accused of practising the *black art*. Bannatyne, the Secretary of Knox, notes in his journal—" On Tuysday the 3d of Julii, 1571, Andro Lundie beand at dener with my maister. in a place of the Lard of Abbotshalls, called Falsyde, openlie affirmet for treuth, that when the queene was lying in ieasing of the king, the Ladie Athole lying thair likwayis, bayth within the Castle of Edinburgh, that he come thair for sum busines, and called for the Ladie Reirres, whom he fand in hir chalmer lying bedfast; and he asking hir of hir disease, sche answrit that sche was never so troubled with no barne that ever sche bair, for the Ladie Athole had cassin all the pyne of her child-birth upon hir."

This countess was Margaret, daughter of Malcolm, third Lord Fleming; the widow of Robert Master of Montrose, and of Thomas Master of Mar, when she gave her hand to the Earl of Athole. The following letter, addressed "To hir sister, my Ladye Livingston," now first printed, may be deemed curious, as the epistle of a witch. The last words and signature only are in the handwriting of the Countess.

"SISTER—Efter maist harty commendationes, for sa mekill as I promest you to adverteis you quhan we var in Stirvelying of my lord's dyet, as I belief he vill not gang out of yis contray quhill Halowmes, and gif my lord zour housband and ze plesis to cum, ze vilbe verray hartly velcum; and my lord my housband desyrs my lord and zow to tak ye pains yrto. Ze vill appardoun me yt I vryt not to zow with my own hand, for ye fit of ane sicknes fallen on my hed, that I can not vryt as ye berar can schow zow. Gif ze meit with my sister ye Ladye Calder, ze vill excuss me yt I vryt not to hir, and yt scho gat not hir aquavyte, for it ran out yt scho suld haif gotten. And gif yr be onye thyng ze wald I did ze vill adverteis. I praye zow faill not to send me my samplar with ye varkp, bath zow put in it, for I haif many warks begun bydand on it. And adverteis me afoir zour cuming in the pairts, that we be not awaye na gaite. Ze will mak my hartye commendation to my lord zour housband, with als meikill of my lords to zour self and him bayth; and God haif (ze) in his kepying. Of Blair ye 23d day of September, 1560, your afficnet and guid sister for ever,
"MARGRET CONTIS OF ATHOLL."

In the case of Margaret Hutchison, a witch, 20th August, 1661, the indictment, among other things, charges, that after her threatenings, Henry Balfour contracted the pains of a woman in child-bed, with a universal swelling in his body, whereof he died. As witches were able to afflict with diseases, so they could transfer them from one person to another, or to four-footed animals, such as dogs and cats. By this traffic they sometimes realised considerable sums. In the Staggering State of Scots Statesmen are the following wonderful anecdotes respecting the family of Mark, commendator of Newbattle, who was master of requests to King James the Sixth, from 1578 to 1597. "He had by his wife, the Lord Herries's daughter, thirty-one children. His lady always kept in her company wise women or witches, and especially one Margaret Nues (Innes), who fostered his daughter, the Lady Borthwick, who was long after his death burnt in Edinburgh for that crime ; and my Lady Lothian's son-in-law, Sir Alexander Hamilton, told one of his friends, how one night lying in Prestongrange, pertaining to the said abbay of Newbottle, he was pulled out of his bed by the said witches, and sore beaten ; of which injury, when he complained to his mother-in-law, and assured her he would complain thereof to the council, she pacified him by giving him a purse full of gold. That lady thereafter, being vexed with a cancer in her breast, implored the help of a notable warlock, by a by-name called Playfair, who condescended to heal her, but with condition, that the sore should fall on them that she loved best; whereunto she agreeing did convalesce; but the earl, her husband, found the boil in his throat, of which he died shortly thereafter; and the said Playfair, being soon apprehended, was made prisoner in Dalkeith steeple, and having confest that and much more wickedness to Mr Archibald Simson, minister there, and that confession coming to the ears of Robert, Earl of Lothian, my lord's son, he had moyen to get some persons admitted to speak with the prisoner in the night, by which means he was found worried in the morning, and the point of his breeches knit about his neck, but never more enquiry was made who had done the deed."

In the legend of Adamsone, archbishop of St. Andrews, a scurrilous pasquil not devoid of humour, we have a list of the charms used by a witch, in order to cure the prelate of a disease, for which the regular practitioners of medicine could discover no remedy.

"He seing weill he wald not mend,
For Phetanissa hes he send,

With sorcerie and incantationes,
Raising the devill with invocationes,
With herbis, stanis, buikis and bellis,
  And south running weilis;
Palme croces, and knottis of strease,
The paring of a priestes auld tees;
And, *in principio*, sought out syne,
That under ane alter of stane had lyne,
Sanct Jhones nutt, and the four levit claver,
With taill and mayn of a baxter aver,
Had careit hame heather to the oyne,
Cutted off in the cruik of the moone;
Halie water, and the lamber beidis,
Hyntworthe, and fourtie uther weidis:
Whairthrow the charming tuik sic force,
They laid it on his fatt whyte horse.
As all men saw, he sone decessit,
Thair Saga slew ane saikles beast."

In this superstitious age, it was not wonderful that even John Knox, the great organ of Reformation, should be esteemed a skilful wizard by the catholics of Scotland. He was accused of attempting to raise *some sanctis* in the churchyard of St. Andrews, among whom Satan himself started up, having a huge pair of horns on his head, at which terrible sight Knox's secretary became mad, and died. Moreover, Nicol Burne, in his Disputation, bitterly inveighs against John as a sorcerer, for having in his old age secured the affections of Lord Ochiltree's daughter, " ane damosil of nobil blude, and he ane auld decrepit creatur of maist bais degree of onie that could be found in the countrey." Certainly such suspicions of philtres and *glamour* are almost warrantable, when it is considered that Knox was the author of "The First Blast of the Trumpet against the monstrous Regiment of Women," in which he most ungallantly affirms, that "nature doth paint them forth to be weak, frail, unpatient, feeble, and foolish; and experience hath declared them to be unconstant, variable, cruel, and void of the spirit of counsel and regiment. For these notable faults, which in all ages have been espied in them, men have not only removed them from rule and authority, but also some have thought that *men subject to the counsel and empire of their wives, were unworthy of all public office.*" At this many ladies of his day would have exclaimed with Sir David Lindsay's Abbasse :—

"How dar thou, carle, presume for till declair,
Or for to mell thee with sa heich mater?
I dar weill say, thou art condempnit in hell,
That dois presume with sic materis to melle;
Fals hureson carle, thou art over arrogant."

But the daughter of Lord Ochiltree could overlook such matrimonial heresy; nay, even the advanced age and harsh features of the reformer were forgotten. His "grim visage of verjuice, scowling over a rusty beard shaped like an otter's tail," had no terrors for her Calvinistic soul; though, in a sense somewhat different from that of Dunbar's *Mariit Woman*, she might have said—

"The luif blenkis of that bogil, fra his bleirit ene,
As Belzebub had on me blent, abasit my spreit."

Knox's visits of gallantry to his mistress, as described by Nicol Burne, form an admirable subject for the comic pencil.

Sir Lewis Ballantyne, Lord Justice-Clerk of Scotland, (1578-1591) " by curiosity, dealt with a warlock, called Richard Grahame, to raise the devil, who having raised him in his own yard in the Canongate, he was thereby so terrified, that he took sickness, and thereof died."—*Staggering State of the Scots Statesmen.*

See the Romance of Sir Tristrem, for the fatal effects of the *boire amoureuse* on that luckless knight and his lady—

"In evil time to sain
The drink was ywrought;"

and the ingenious note on the passage. Scott of Scotstarvet informs us, that the first Lord Balmerino, "being a widower, got an amatorious potion from a maid in his house, called Young, (thereafter wife to Dr. Honeyman) of which he died." For "the toies, which are said to procure love," as Reginald Scott terms them, consult his Discovery of Witchcraft, b. 6. c. 7.

At the same period, witches abounded in all parts of Scotland. Knox particularly mentions the Countess of Huntley as a patroness of these hags. Giving an account of the skirmish of Corrichie, in which her husband died from fatigue, he says :—" The erle, immediately after his taiking, depairted this lyif without ony wound, or yit appeirance of ony straick, quhairof death mycht have ensewed; and so, becaus it was lait, he was cast over athort a pair of creilles, and so was caried to Aberdene, and was layd in the Tolboyth thareof, that the respons quhilk his wyif's witches had gevin, mycht be fulfilled, quha all affirmed, (as the most pairt say) that that same nycht sould he be in the Tolboyth of Aberdene, without ony wound upon his body. Quhen his lady gat knowledge theirof, sche blaimit hir principall witch, called Jonet; bot sche stoutly defendit hirself, (as the devill can evir do) and affirmed, that sche gave a trew answer, albeit, sche spack not all the treuth, for sche knew that he sould be thare dead; bot that culd not profit my lady, sche was angry and sorry for a season; bot the devill, the mess, and witches, have als gritt credit of hir this day, the 12th of Junii,

1566, as they had sevin yeirs ago." The son of this Lord Huntly, George, the fifth earl, died suddenly in a convulsion fit, as it would appear, attended with several uncommon symptoms. A very curious account of his death has been printed by Mr. Dalyell, at the end of Bannatyne's Journal. Several of his followers, the narrator affirms, were seized with a disorder resembling that of the earl, whose corpse, being removed to the chapel before inhumation, the chamber in which it was embalmed, was haunted with "ane greit noys and din; whidder it was of speiche, of grayning, or rumbling, I can not tell."

In the journal prefixed to this narrative, there is mention of a very notable witch burnt at St. Andrews in the year 1572, who declared openly that she cared not whether she went to heaven or hell. A white cloth, "like a collore craig with stringis, whairon was mony knottis," being taken from about her person, she immediately gave way to despair, exclaiming, "Now I have no hoip of myself." In the Historie of King James the Sext, the regent of Scotland is said to have repaired to St. Andrews (May 1569), "quhair a notabill sorceres callit Nicniven, (this name, generally given to the Queen of the Fairies, was probably bestowed upon her on account of her crimes,) was condemmit to the death and burnt." This I suspect to be the witch above-mentioned, though the dates disagree. The author of the historie adds, "a Frenchman callit Paris, quha was ane of the designeris of the king's death, was hangit in St. Andro, and with him William Steward, lyoun king of armes, for divers pointes of witchcraft and necromancie."

In the year 1588, Alison Pearson, in Byre-hills, Fifeshire, was convicted of practising sorcery, and of invoking the foul fiend; she acknowledged that she had been intimate with the Queen of Elfland for many years, and that she had many friends of her own kin in the Court of Fairy. Her extravagant confession may be found in the Border Minstrelsy, vol. ii. p. 213. Two years afterwards, Catharine Ross, Lady Fowllis, was endited at the instance of the king's advocate, and Hector Munro of Foullis, her own son-in-law, for witchcraft. The first article of accusation urged against her is "the making of two clay pictures, one for the destruction of the young Lady Balnagowan, and getting them enchanted, and shooting of elf-arrow heads at the saids persons; second, for making a stoupfull of poisoned aill for performance of your devillish malice, wherewith ye killed sundry; third, sending a pigfull of poyson to the house where young Foullis was, the carrier whereof falling, and with the fall breaking the pig, and seeing the liquor, tasted it, and dyed immediately; and the grasse which grows where it fell, no beast will eat of it; fourth, for saying that ye would use all means that may be had of God in heaven, or the devill in hell, for destroying Marjory Campbell, the Lady Balnagowan, that the laird might marry the lady Foullis; also hindering a commission that was granted for tryall of witches, and procuring a suspension thereof, which, if thou had been ane honest woman, thou would never have done."—*Abbreviate of the Justiciary Record.* It appears that the Lady of Foullis, together with Christian Ross, and other witches, had made two clay images, one representing Robert Munro, then fiar of Foullis, the other Marjory Campbell, spouse to Ross, younger of Balnagowan; but these figures chancing to break, one of the witches undertook, at Lady Foullis's desire, to compose two more, which accordingly was done. This Christian Ross, who was burnt for the crime at Channerie, confessed her guilt before Urquhart of Cromarty, and Irvine of Kynnock. And William Macgillimondan, a *warlock*, who also suffered death for the same practices, confessed the acts of poison, particularly an attempt to destroy the chief of the name of Munro. These hags and wizards sometimes composed their enchanted figures of butter. Lady Foullis was acquitted, as was also her husband, Hector Munro of Foullis, accused of "consulting of witches in order to cure his brother of sicknesse, and to cure himself; and that the said witches came to him, and practised their devillish charms, particularly that one of them dug a grave on the confines of lands belonging to two different superiors, in which they laid him, and after using several devillish charms, took him up, by which means he was recovered, and the disease laid upon George Munro, son to Katharine Ross, Lady Fowles, of which he dyed."

The next remarkable trial for witchcraft in the Justiciary Record (1590) is that of Bessy Roy, servant to the Laird of Boquhane, who, among other magical performances, " once in the field, in the presence of sundry other servants, drew a compas, made a hole in the midst of it; then, by her conjurations, came forth a great worme, and crap over the circle; then a small one, and also crap over; then a great one, which sank again into the hole; which enchantment she interpreted thus to them: The first great worm is the goodman, that he shall live long; the second is a barne in the ladye's womb, (whereas nobody knew she was with barne,) and that the barne should live; the last great worme was the goodwyfe, that should die of the birth; all which came to pass as she said."

CHAPTER III.

(A.D. 1591 to A.D. 1593.)

The Famous Doctor Fian and his Associates—Their Doings and Trial—Doctor Fian's Confession—His Escape and Recapture—Put to the Torture—Burned on the Castle Hill.

BUT about this time a wonderful conspiracy of Satan's agents was discovered near to Edinburgh, the circumstances of which are given in a very scarce black-letter pamphlet, entitled,—" Newes from Scotland, declaring the damnable Life of Doctor Fian, a notable Sorcerer, who was burned at Edenbrough in Januarie last, 1591; which Doctor was Register to the Devill, that sundrie times Preached at North-Baricke Kirke to a number of notorious Witches. With the true Examinations of the said Doctor and Witches, as they uttered them in the presence of the Scottish King; discovering how they pretended to Bewitch and Drowne his Majestie in the sea coming from Denmarke, with such other wonderful Matters as the like hath not bin heard at anie time. Published according to the Scottish Copie. Printed for William Wright." After an address to the reader, in which the pamphleteer observes, that he was principally induced to print a narrative of these wonders, "for that sundrie written coppies are lately dispersed thereof, containing that the said witches were first discovered by means of a poore pedlar, travelling in the town of Tranent, and that by a wonderfull manner hee was in a moment convayed at midnight from Scotland to Burdeux, in France, (being places of no small distance) into a merchante's sellar there (see Appendix, note 1); and after being sent from Burdeux into Scotland by certain Scottish merchants, to the king's majestie, that he discovered those witches, and was the cause of their apprehension; with a number of matters miraculous and incredible, all which, in truth, are most false," he makes some observations on the merciful interposition of Providence with regard to the wicked designs of the sorcerers and witches, and then proceeds to state, that " within the town of Trenent, in the kingdome of Scotland, there dwelleth one David Seaton, who being deputie bailiffe in the said towne, had a maide called Geillis Duncane, who used secretlie to absent and lie forth of her maister's house every other night. This Geillis Duncane tooke in hand to helpe all such as were troubled or grieved with anie kind of sickness or infirmitie, and in short space did perfourme many matters most miraculous; which things, for asmuch as she began to do them upon a sodaine, having never done the like before, made her maister and others to be in great admiration, and wondered thereat; by means wherof the saide David Seaton had his maide in greate suspition that she did not those things by natural and lawfull waies, but rather supposed it to bee done by some extraordinarie and unlawful meanes.

"Whereupon her maister began to grow verie inquisitive, and examined hir which way, and by what meanes, shee was able to performe matters of so great importance? whereat shee gave him no answere. Nevertheless, her maister, to the intent that hee might the better trie and finde out the truth of the same, did, with the help of others, torment her with the torture of the pilliwinkes upon her fingers, which is a grievous torture, and binding or wrinching her head with a cord or roape, which is a most cruell torment also, yet would she not confess anie thing; whereuppon they suspecting that she had been marked by the devill, (as commonly witches are) made diligent search about her, and found the enemies mark to be in her fore crag, or fore part of her throate (see Appendix, note 2); which being found, shee confessed that all her doings was done by the wicked allurements and entisements of the devil, and that she did them by witchcraft.

"After this her confession, she was committed to prison, where she continued a season, where immediately she accused these persons following to bee notorious witches, and caused them forthwith to be apprehended, one after another, viz.—Agnes Sampson, the eldest witch of them all, dwelling in Haddington; Agnes Tompson, of Edinbrough; Doctor Fian, *alias* John Cunningham, master of the schoole at Saltpans, in Lowthian, of whose life and strange acts you shal heare more largely in the end of this discourse. These were by the saide Geillis Duncane accused, as also George Mott's wife, dwelling in Lowthian; Robert Grierson, skipper; and Jennet Blandilands; with the potter's wife of Seaton; the smith at the Brigge Hallis; with innumerable others in those parts, and dwelling in those bounds aforesaid, of whom some are alreadie executed; the rest remaine in prison, to receive the doome of judgement at the king's majesties will and pleasure.

"The said Geillis Duncane also caused Ewphame Mecalrean to bee apprehended, who conspired and performed the death of her god-father, and who used her art upon a gentleman being one of the lordes and justices of the session, for bearing good will to her daughter. She also caused to be apprehended one Barbara Naper, for bewitchinge to death Archibalde, the last Earle of Angus, who languished to death by witchcraft, and yet the same was not suspected, but that hee died of so straunge a disease as the phisition

knewe not how to cure or remedie the same.
But of all other the saide witches, these two last
before-recited, were reputed for as civill honest
women as anie that dwelled within the cittie of
Edenbrough, before they were apprehended.
Many other besides were taken, dwelling in
Leith, who are detayned in prison untill his
majesties further will and pleasure be knowne :
of whose wicked dooings you shall particularly
heare, which was as followeth :

"This aforesaide Agnis Sampson, which was
the elder witch, was taken and brought to Hali-
riud-House, before the king's majestie, and sundry
other of the nobilitie of Scotland, where she was
straytly examined, but all the perswasions which
the king's majestie used to hir, with the rest of
his councell, might not provoke or induce her to
confesse any thing, but stoode stiffely in the
deniall of all that was layde to her charge; whereupon they caused her to bee conveyed away unto
prison, there to receive such torture as hath beene
lately provided for witches in that country....

"*Item.* The sayde Agnis Sampson was after
brought againe before the king's majestie and his
councell, and being examined of the meetings and
detestable dealings of those witches, shee confessed
that upon the night of Allhollon-Even, shee was
accompanied, as well with the persons aforesaide,
as also with a great many other witches, to the

number of two hundreth, and that all they together went to sea, each one in a riddle, or cive, and went in the same very substantially, with flaggons of wine, making merrie and drinking by the way in the same riddles or cives, to the kirke of North-Barrick, in Lowthian, and that after they had landed, tooke handes on the lande, and daunced this reill, or short daunce, singing all with one voice :—

"Commer, goe ye before, commer, goe ye;
Gif ye will not goe before, commer, let me."

At which time shee confessed, that this Geillis Duncane did goe before them, playing this reill or daunce uppon a small trumpe, called a Jewe's trump, untill they entered into the Kerk of North Barrick.

"These confessions made the king in a wonderfull admiration, and sent for the saide Geillis Duncane, who, upon the like trump, did play the saide daunce before the kinges majestie, who, in respect of the strangenes of these matters, tooke great delight to be present at their examinations. *Item*, the said Agnis Sampson confessed that the divell being then at North Barrick Kerke, attending their comming, in the habit or likenesse of a man, and seeing that they tarried over long, hee at their comming enjoyned them all to a pennance, which was, that they should kisse his buttockes, in sign of duety to him, which being put over the pulpit bare, every one did as he had enjoyned them; and having made his ungodly exhortations, wherein he did greatly inveigh against the King of Scotland, he received their oathes for their good and true service towards him, and departed; which done, they returned to sea, and so home againe.

"At which time the witches demanded of the divell, Why he did beare such hatred to the king? who answered, by reason the king is the greatest enemie hee hath in the world. All which their confessions and depositions are still extant upon record.

"*Item*, The saide Agnes Sampson confessed before the king's majestie sundrie thinges, which were so miraculous and strange, as that his majestie saide they were all extreame lyars; whereat shee aunswered, she would not wish his majestie to suppose her wordes to be false, but rather to beleve them, in that she would discover such matter unto him as his majestie should not any way doubt of.

"And thereupon, taking his majestie a little aside, shee declared unto him the verie wordes which passed betweene the kinges majestie and his queene at Upslo, in Norway, the first night of mariage, with their answere ech to other; wherat the kinges majestie wondered greatly, and swore by the living God that he believed that all the devils in hell could not have discovered the same, acknowledging her words to be most true, and therefore gave the more credit to the rest that is before declared.

"Touching this Agnis Sampson, she is the only woman who, by the divel's perswasion, should have intended and put in execution the kinges majesties death in this manner.

"Shee confessed that shee tooke a blacke toade, and did hang the same up by the heeles three daies, and collected and gathered the venom as it dropped and fell from it in an oister-shell, and kept the same venome close covered, until she should obtaine anie parte or peece of foule linnen cloth that had appertained to the king's majestie, as shirt, handkercher, napkin, or any other thing, which shee practised to obtaine by meanes of one John Kers, who being attendant in his majesties chamber, desired him, for olde acquaintaunce betweene them, to helpe her to one, or a peece of such a cloth as is aforesaide, which thing the said John Kers denyed to help her to, saying hee could not help her unto it.

"And the saide Agnis Sampson, by her depositions since her apprehension, saith, that if shee had obtained any one peece of linnen cloth which the king had worne and fowled, she had bewitched him to death, and put him to such extraordinary paines as if he had been lying upon sharp thorns and endes of needles.

"Moreover, she confessed that at the time when his majestie was in Denmarke, shee being accompanied with the parties before specially named, tooke a cat and christened it, and afterward bound to each part of that cat the cheefest parte of a dead man, and severall joyntes of his bodie; and that in the night following, the said cat was convayed into the middest of the sea by all these witches, sayling in their riddles or cives, as is aforesaid, and so left the saide cat right before the towne of Leith, in Scotland; this doone, there did arise such a tempest in the sea, as a greater hath not bene seene, which tempest was the cause of the perishing of a boat or vessell comming over from the towne of Brunt Island to the towne of Leith, wherein was sundrie jewelles and rich giftes, which should have beene presented to the new queene of Scotland, at her majesties coming to Leith.

"Againe it is confessed, that the said christened cat was the cause that the kinges majesties shippe, at his comming forth of Denmarke, had a contrarie winde to the rest of his shippes then being in his companie, which thing was most straunge and true, as the kinges majestie acknowledgeth; for when the rest of the shippes had a faire and good winde, then was the winde contrarie and altogether against his majestie. And further, the sayde witch declared, that his majestie had never come safely from the sea, if his faith had not prevayled above their intentions.

"As touching the aforesaide Doctor Fian, *alias* John Cunningham, the examination of his actes since his apprehension, declareth the great subteltie of the divell, and therefore maketh thinges to appeare the more miraculous; for being apprehended by the accusation of the saide Geillis Duncane aforesaid, who confessed he was their regester, and that there was not one man suffered to come to the divel's readinges but onelie hee. The said doctor was taken and imprisoned, and used with the accustomed paine provided for those offences inflicted upon the rest, as is aforesaid.

"First, by thrawing of his head with a rope, whereat he would confesse nothing.

"Secondly, he was perswaded by faire meanes to confesse his follies, but that would prevaile as little.

"Lastly, hee was put to the most severe and cruell paine in the world, called the bootes, who, after he had received three strokes, being inquired if he would confesse his damnable actes and wicked life, his toong would not serve him to speake; in respect whereof, the rest of the witches willed to search his toong, under which was founde two pinnes thrust up into the heade whereupon the witches did say, now is the charme stinted, and shewed that those charmed pins were the cause he could not confesse any thing; then was he immediately released of the bootes, brought before the king, his confession was taken, and his own hand willingly set thereunto, which contained as followeth:

"First, That at the generall meetings of those witches, he was always present: That he was clarke to all those that were in subjection to the divel's service bearing the name of witches: That alway hee did take their oathes for their true service to the divell, and that he wrote for them such matters as the divell still pleased to commaund him.

"*Item*, Hee confessed that by his witchcraft hee did bewitch a gentleman dwelling neere to the Saltpans, where the said doctor kept schoole, onely for being enamoured of a gentlewoman whome hee loved himselfe; by meanes of which his sorcery, witchcraft, and divelish practices, hee caused the said gentleman that once in twenty-four howers he fell into a lunacie and madnes, and so continued one whole hower together; and for the veritie of the same hee caused the gentleman to bee brought before the king's majestie, which was uppon the twenty-third day of December last; and being in his majesties chamber, suddenly hee gave a great scritch, and fell into madnesse, sometimes bending himselfe and sometime capring so directly up, that his heade did touch the seeling of the chamber, to the great admiration of his majestie, and others then present, so that all the gentlemen in the chamber were not able to hold him until they called in more helpe, who together bound him hand and foot; and suffering the saide gentleman to lie still untill his furie were past, he, within an hower, came againe to himselfe, when being demaunded of the king's majestie, what he saw or did all that while? answered, That he had been in a sound sleepe.

"*Item*, The said Doctor did also confesse, that hee had used means sundry times to obtaine his purpose and wicked intent of the same gentle-woman, and seeing himselfe disappointed of his intention, he determined, by all wayes hee might, to obtaine the same, trusting by conjuring, witchcraft, and sorcerie, to obtaine it in this manner."

The author proceeds to state, that the Doctor employed one of his scholars, a brother of the young lady, to procure three of her hairs, by which he might bewitch her to his wicked purposes, giving the boy a piece of conjured paper wherein to deposit them; but some suspicious circumstances alarmed the mother, " by reason she was a witch of herself, and was very inquisitive of the boy to understand his intent, and the better to know the same, did beate him with sundrie stripes, whereby he discovered the truth unto her. The mother, therefore, being well practised in witchcraft, did thinke it most convenient to meete with the Doctor in his owne arte, and thereupon took the paper from the boy, wherein hee should have put the same haires, and went to a young heyfer which never had borne calfe, and with a paire of sheeres clipped off three haires from the udder of the cow, and wrapt them in the same paper, which shee againe delivered to the boy, then willing him to give the same to his said maister, which he immediately did.

" The schoolmaister, so soone as he had received them, thinking them indeed to be the maid's haires, went straight and wrought his arte upon them; but the Doctor had no sooner doone his intent to them but presently the heyfer cow, whose haires they were indeede, came unto the doore of the church wherein the schoolemaister was, into the which the heyfer went, and made towards the schoolmaister, leaping and dauncing upon him, and following him forth of the church, and to what place soever he went, to the great admiration of all the townesmen of Saltpans, and many other who did beholde the same.

"The report whereof made all men imagine that he did worke it by the divell, without whome it could never have beene so sufficiently effected; and thereupon the name of the said Doctor Fian (who was but a very yoong man) began to growe so common among the people of Scotland, that he was secretly nominated for a notable conjurer.

"All which although in the beginning he denied, and would not confesse, yet having felt the pain of the bootes, (and the charme stinted, as aforesayd), he confessed all the aforesaid to be most true, without producing anie witnesses to justifie the same, and therupon, before the king's majesty, he subscribed the sayd confessions with his owne hande, which, for truth, remaineth upon record in Scotland.

"After that the depositions and examinations of the sayd Doctor Fian, *alias* Cuningham, was taken, as already is declared, with his own hand willingly set thereunto, hee was, by the master of the prison, committed to ward, and appointed to a chamber by himself, where, forsaking his wicked wayes, acknowledging his most ungodly lyfe, shewing that he had too much folowed the allurements and entisements of Sathan, and fondly practised his conclusions by conjuring, witchcraft, inchantment, sorcerie, and such like, hee renounced the devill and all his wicked workes, vowed to leade the life of a Christian, and seemed newly converted towards God.

"The morrow after, upon conference had with him, he granted that the devill had appeared unto him in the night before, appareled all in blacke, with a white wand in his hande, and that the devill demanded of him if hee would continue his faithfull service, according to his first oath and promise made to that effect, whome (as hee then said) he utterly renounced to his face, and said unto him, in this manner, 'Avoide, Satan, avoide, for I have listened too much unto thee, and by the same thou hast undone me, in respect whereof I utterly forsake thee." To whom the devill answered, 'That once, ere thou die, thou shalt be mine; and with that (as he sayd) the devill brake the white wand, and immediately vanished foorth of his sight.'

"Thus all the daie this Doctor Fian continued verie solitarie, and seemed to have a care of his owne soule, and would call uppon God, shewing himselfe penitent for his wicked life; neverthelesse, the same night, hee found such meanes that hee stole the key of the prison doore and chamber in the which he was, which, in the night, hee opened and fled awaie to the Saltpans, where hee was alwayes resident, and first apprehended; of whose sodaine departure, when the king's majestie had intelligence, hee presently commanded diligent inquirie to bee made for his apprehension; and for the better effecting thereof, hee sent publicke proclamations into all partes of his lande to the same effect, by meanes of whose hot and harde pursuite, he was agayn taken and brought to prison, and then being called before the king's highnes, he was re-examined as well touching his departure, as also touching all that had before happened.

"But this Doctor, notwithstanding that his owne confession appeareth remaining in recorde under his owne hande-writing, and the same thereunto fixed in the presence of the king's majestie, and sundrie of his councell, yet did he utterly denie the same.

"Whereupon the kinges majestie perceiving his stubbourne wilfulnesse, conceived and imagined that in the time of his absence hee had entered into newe conference and league with the devill, his master, and that hee had beene agayne newly marked, for the which he was narrowly searched, but it coulde not in anie wice be founde; yet, for more tryall of him to make him confesse, hee was commaunded to have a most straunge torment, which was done in this manner following:—

"His nailes upon all his fingers were riven and pulled off with an instrument called in Scottish a turkas, which in England wee call a payre of pincers, and under everie nayle there was thrust in two needles over, even up to the heads; at all which tormentes, notwithstanding, the Doctor never shronke anie whit, neither woulde he then confesse it the sooner for all the tortures inflicted upon him.

"Then was hee, with all convenient speed, by commandement, convaied againe to the torment of the bootes, wherein he continued a long time, and did abide so many blowes in them, that his legges were crusht and beaten together as small as might bee, and the bones and flesh so bruised, that the blood and marrow spouted forth in great abundance, whereby they were made unserviceable for ever; and notwithstanding all these grievous paines and cruell torments, hee would not confess anie things; so deeply had the devill entered into his heart, that hee utterly denied all that which he had before avouched, and would saie nothing therunto but this, that what he had done and sayde before, was onely done and sayde for fear of paynes which he had endured.

"Upon great consideration, therefore, taken by the king's majestie and his counsell, as well for the due execution of justice upon such detestable malefactors, as also for example sake, to remayne a terrour to all others hereafter, that shall attempt to deale in the lyke wicked and ungodlye actions, as witchcraft, sorcery, conjuration, and such lyke, the sayde Doctor Fian was soone after arraigned, condemned, and adjudged by the law to die, and then to bee burned, according to the lawe of that lande, provided in that behalfe. Whereupon hee was put into a carte, and being first strangled, he was immediately put into a great fire, being readie provided for that purpose, and there burned in the Castle-hill of Edenbrough, on a Saterdaie, in the ende of Januarie last past, 1591.

"The rest of the witches which are not executed, remayne in prison till farther triall, and knowledge of his majesties pleasure."

Regarding the three females, Euphame Maccalzeane, Barbara Napier, and Agnes Sampson, referred to in the preceding, the following give some information :—" Euphame Maccalzeane, (her father was ane advocate) spouse to Patrick Maccalzeane, *alias* Moscropt, for many treasonable conspiracies undertaken by witchcraft, to have destroyed the king's person by a pictur of wax, and have bereft his majesty of his life. *Item*, for enterprysing to kill her husband, that she might gett another goodman, and for drowning a boat betwixt Leith and Kinghorne, wherein were 60 persons lost; convict of thir, and many other monstrous points, sentenced to be burnt quick to the death, and all hir lands and goods forfaulted." —Fountainhall's *MS. Abstract of the Justiciary Record.* This woman was possessed of a considerable estate in her own right, being the daughter of Thomas M'Calzeane, Lord Cliftonhall, one of the senators of the College of Justice, who died in the year 1581; it appears, however, that there were doubts as to the legitimacy of her birth.—Spottiswoode's *Practicks*, p. 219. Her children were restored by act of parliament (1592) against the forfeiture, after paying five thousand marks to the donator, of escheat, and relinquishing the estate of Cliftonhall, which the king gave to Sir James Sandilands of Slamanno.

"Barbara Napier, spouse to Archibald Douglas, burges of Edinburgh, for witchcraft, as consulting with Richard Grahame, a notorious necromancer, how to keip Dame Jean Lyon, Lady Angus, from vomiting when she was breiding hir barnes, and giving him 3 elles of bombezie for his paynes, and such other poynts of witchcraft, so that her ditty seems to me to be rather for seiking after witches and sorcerers, for knowing how to do things, than for being a witch herself. She was convict and burnt."—Fountainhall's *MS*. Hume of Godscroft, in his Account of Archibald, ninth Earl of Angus, says,—"His death (anno 1588) was ascribed to witchcraft; and one Barbary Nepair, in Edinburgh, wife to Archibald Douglas, of the house of Cashogle, was apprehended on suspicion, but I know not whether she was convicted of it or not; only it was reported that she was found guiltie, and that the execution was deferred because she was with childe, but afterwards, nobody insisting in the pursuit of her, she was set at libertie." It appears that Agnes Sampson was also concerned in the plot against the life of Angus, who, according to Spottiswoode, obstinately refused the aid of Richard Grahame, the wizard mentioned above, by whose skill he might have counteracted the charms of the witches. "Anna Simson, (*i. e.* Agnes Sampson) a famous witch," continues Godscroft, "is reported to have confessed at her death that a picture of waxe was brought to her, having A. D. written on it, which (as they said to her) did signifie Archibald Davidson, and shee not thinking of the Earl of Angus, whose name was Archibald Douglas, and might have been called Davidson, because his father's name was David, did consecrate, or execrate it, after her forme, which, she said, if she had knowne to have represented him, shee would not have done it for all the world." It appears wonderful enough, from the very suspicious intercourse between these hags and Lady Angus, (whose great-grandmother, Lady Glammis, seems to have been brought to the stake on more slender presumptions for witchcraft) that the countess herself escaped a criminal prosecution. She was the widow of Robert Douglas, younger of Lochleven, when Lord Angus, after divorcing his second wife, a daughter of Lord

Rothes, for adultery, married her in the year 1586. Having buried her second husband, her wealth attracted a third, Alexander Lindsay, afterwards Lord Spynie, a youthful favourite of King James the Sixth, who is said to have addressed the following very laconic admonitory epistle to Lindsay from Denmark:—" Deir Sandie,—Wee are going on heir in the auld way, and verrie merrie. I'll not forget yow whan I come hame; you sall be a lord. But mynd Jean Lyon, for her auld tout will mack yow a new horne."

Agnes Sampson, commonly called the wise wife of Keith, concerning whom Spottiswoode, p. 383, relates a story not confirmed by the record, confessed to the king himself, that on one occasion " the devil, in man's likeness, met her going out to the fields from her own house at Keith, betwixt five and six at even, being alone, and commanded her to be at North-Berwick Kirk the next night, to which place she came on horseback, conveyed by her good-son, called John Couper, and lighted at the Kirk-yard, or a little before she came to it, about eleven hours at even. They danced along the kirk-yard, Geillie Duncan playing on a trump, (Jew's harp) and John Fian, muzzled, (masked) led the ring. The said Agnes and her daughter followed next; besides, there were Kate Gray, Robert Grierson, &c., with the rest of their kimmers, above 100 persons, whereof there were six men, and all the rest women. The women made first their courtesy to their master, and then the men; the men turning nine times widdershins about, and the women six times. John Fian blew up the kirk doors, and blew in the lights, which were like meikle black candles stiking round about the pulpit. The devil himself started up in the pulpit like a meikle black man, and calling the row, every one answered,—Here. Mr. Robert Grierson being named, they all ran hirdie-girdie, and were angry, for it was promised that he should be called Robert the Comptroller, for the expriming of his name. "The devil then preached a sermon, after which they rifled three graves for magical cookery. Agnes got for her part a winding-sheet and two joints. John Fian, *alias* Cunninghame, who, Agnes said, was ever nearest to the devil, *at his left elbock*, confessed that he was carried 'in an extasie' to the kirk at North Berwick, where the devil preached to them, bidding them not spare to do evil; to eat, drink, and be merriye, for he should raise them all up gloriously at the last day; that Satan pointed out certain graves, which were opened, and he saw the women dismember the corpses with *gullies*. The devil taught them to baptize a cat, and throw it into the sea, calling Hola! which would raise a storm to shipwreck the king; and on John's attempting to catch a cat for that purpose, and she proving very nimble, he was carried about in the air after her in a wonderful manner. Also, on his majesty's return, Satan raised a mist, by throwing something like a foot-ball into the sea, and this was done that James might be cast upon the English shore. Fian also confessed, that earnestly wishing to be revenged on a neighbour of his, the devil, for the first time, appeared to him in white raiment, and told him, that if he would serve and adore him, he should never want for any thing, and be revenged on all his enemies; and that Satan threatened to desert him, and do him mischief when he was going to marry."—*Justiciary Record.* Agnes Sampson's indictment consists of 53 points, most of which concern her curing of diseases, ascertaining whether these were natural or devilish, brought on by witchcraft and elf-arrows, and using a prayer said to be devilish; "whilk prayer she learnit frae hir fadder," by which she foreknew if the person whom she desired to cure would live or die; for if she stopt in repeating it, it was a token of the patient's death. The prayer she said was this:—

I trow in Almighty God, that wrought baith
    heaven and earth, and all of nocht;
Into his dearest son, Christ Jesus, into that
    comely Lord I trow

Wes gotten of the Holy Ghaist, born of the Virgin Mary;
Stepped to heaven, that all weill then, and sitts at his Father's right hand.
He bad us come, and their to dome, both quick and dead to him conveine;
I trow also in the Haly Ghaist, in haly kirk my hope is maist;
That haly ship wheir hallowers winns to ask forgivenes of their sinnes,
And syne to ryse in flesch and bane, the life that never mair hes gane.
Thou sayds Lord loved may ye be, that formed and made mankind of me;
Thou cust me on the haly croce, thou lent me body, saull, and voce,
And ordained me to heaven's blisse, wherfore I thank the Lord of this.
That all your hallowers loved be, to pray to them to pray to me;
And keep me from that fellon sea, and from the sin that saull would slay;
Thou, Lord, for thy bitter passion, to keep me fra sin and worldly shame,
And endless damnation, grant me the joy never will be gane.
    Sweit Jesus Christus, Amen.

"*Item*, She went with the witch of Carreburn, and other witches, to the Kirk of Newton, and taking up dead folks and jointing them, made enchanted powders for witchcraft. *Item*, She went with other witches in a boat, the devil going before them like a rock of hay. *Item*, The devil, in the shape of a dog, gave her responses concerning her laird's recovery, and endeavoured to put awa ane of the ladies daughters. *Item*, She raised a universal great storm in the sea when the queen was coming to Scotland, and wrote a letter to that effect to a witch in Leith. *Item* She used this prayer in healing of sicknesse:—

All kynds of ill that ever may be, in Christ's
    name I conjure thee,
I conjure thee baith mare and lesse, with all the
    vertues of the messe,
And right sa with the naills sa, that nailed Jesus
    and na ma,
And right sa by the samen bluid that raiked our
    the ruthfull ruid,
Furth of the flech and of the bane, and in the
    eird and in the stane,
        I conjure thee in God's name."——

For more such like doggrel, see the chapter "Anent some Prayers, Charms, and Aves, used in the Highlands," in Satan's Invisible World, and The Wonderful Discoverie of Witches in the Countie of Lancaster, 1613.

Francis Earl of Bothwell, whose restless spirit gave King James so much uneasiness, was accused by these witches of consulting them respecting his sovereign's fate, and of having employed their art in raising the storms at sea which endangered the queen's life, and impeded James's return from Denmark. His imprisonment and subsequent enterprises are well known. But we learn from Sandys, that in his last retreat the earl himself was esteemed a skilful necromancer. Talking of Calabria, in the year 1610, he says,—" Here a certain Calabrian, hearing that I was an Englishman, came to me, and would needs persuade me that I had insight in magick, for that Earl Bothwell was my countryman, who lives at Naples, and is in those parts famous for suspected necromancy." See Mr. Robert Bruce's Sermons, for a curious discourse preached at Edinburgh, 9th November, 1589.—" At the which time the Earle Bothwell made his publicke repentance in the church,"—Part of the text probably alludes to his magical propensities,—" and put away foolish and unlearned questions, knowing that they ingender strife."—Second Epistle to Tim. c. ii. His son, whom Lilly styles Lord Bothwell, though the title is said never to have been restored, seems to have inherited his father's turn for metaphysical intercourse. Lilly, talking of one Evans, an astrologer, and a Welshman, a drunkard, and seldom without a black eye, who principally subsisted on the sale of antimonial cups, says,—" Some time before I became acquainted with him, he then living in the Minories, was desired by the Lord Bothwell, and Sir Kenelm Digby, to show them a spirit. He promised so to do; the time came, and they were all in the body of the circle, when, lo, upon the sudden, after some time of invocation, Evans was taken from out the room, and carried into the field near Battersea Causeway, close to the Thames. Next morning a countryman going by to his labour, and espying a man in black cloaths came unto him and awaked him, and asked him, how he came there? Evans by this understood his condition, enquired where he was, how far from London, and in what parish he was? which, when he understood, he told the labourer, he had been late at Battersea the night before, and by chance was left there by his friends. Sir Kenelm Digby, and the Lord Bothwell, went home without any harm, came next day to hear what was become of him; just as they, in the afternoon, came into the house, a messenger came from Evans to his wife, to come to him at Battersea. I enquired, upon what account the spirit carried him away? who said, he had not, at the time of invocation, made any suffumigation, at which the spirits were vexed."—*Life and Times*, p. 32.

CHAPTER IV.

(A.D. 1594 to A.D. 1629.)

The Earl of Argyle's Witch—The Countess of Arran deceived—Alison Balfour the Orkney Witch—James V. and his "Dæmonologie"—The Earl of Gowrie and the Enchanted Parchment—The Murder of Kincaid—The Devil at Corstorphine—Lawrie Burned on the Castle Hill—The Burning of Isobel Grierson and Barbara Paterson—Curing and Inflicting Diseases.

IN the "Faithful Narrative of the Great and Miraculous Victory obtained by George Gordon, Earl of Huntly, and Francis Hay, Earl of Errol, Catholic Noblemen, over Archibald Campbell, Earl of Argyle, Lieutenant, at Strathaven, in the North of Scotland, 3d October, 1594," Argyle is accused of having been "accompanied by a noted witch, on purpose to discover the property and hidden treasures of the inhabitants, by her incantations; which," says the narrator, "notwithstanding they injured others, did us no harm, for when she raised a thick mist to confound our eyes, as we absolutely saw, it immediately failed, there being something in our camp, she said, after she was taken, that greatly impeded her exertions, &c. The enchantress of whom I have spoken, delivered oracles to Argyle worthy a Pythian spirit; one of her prophecies was, that on the following Friday, which was the day after the battle, Argyle's harp should be played in Buchan; and the bagpipe, which is the principal military instrument of the Scottish mountaineers, should sound in Strathbogie, Huntly's seat. Nor were her vaticinations entirely vain; for both the harp and bagpipe sounded in Strathbogie and Turef; but the general was not there to enjoy their most agreeable music; neither could her sorcery foresee the death that awaited her after the victory." A few years posterior to this event, the celebrated wife of Captain James Stewart, Earl of Arran, was still more grossly deceived by the hypothetical predictions of these treacherous slaves to the false spirit. "She got a response from the witches, that she should be the greatest woman in Scotland, and that her husband should have the highest head in that kingdom. Both which fell out; for she died, being all swelled out in an extraordinary manner; and he, riding to the south, was pursued by the Lord Torthoral, (called Douglas,) whose whole family the said Captain James intended to have extirpated, and was killed, and his head carried on the point of a spear till it was brought to a church-yard. After which time the Hamiltons were restored to their own estate of Arran."—*Staggering State*, p. 9. The last of this branch of the family of Ochiltree was William Lord Ochiltree, who died at the University of Edinburgh in the year 1675, aged sixteen. He is mentioned in a MS. History of the Lairds of Garthland, as "the boy that was so celebrate for his vein and genius of poetry;" but his fame seems to have been nearly as brief as his existence. Sir James Douglas of Parkhead, above-mentioned, styled Lord Tothorwald, as having married the heiress of that barony, was afterwards run through the body, on the High Street of Edinburgh, by a nephew of Captain James Stewart, and died without uttering one word. On clearing away the rubbish which till lately covered the pavement of the Chapel at Holyrood-House, his tombstone was found, with this mutilated inscription:—"Heir lyes ane nobil and potent Lord James Douglas—and Cairlell and Torthorall, wha mariet Daime Elizabeth Cairlell, air and heretrix yr of, wha was slaine in Edinburgh ye 14 day of July, in ye zeir of God 1608—vas slaine in 48."

On the 24th of June, 1596, John Stewart, master of Orkney, was indicted for consulting with Alison Balfour, a witch, for the destruction of Patrick Earl of Orkney, his brother, by poison. He gave in a written declaration by way of defence, stating, among other things, that no regard ought to be paid to the confession of the witch, as it was extorted by various torments. The following document is produced to confirm this assertion:—"*Apud* Kirkwall, upon the Heding Hill

of the same, the saxtene day of December, 1594,
in presence of Thomas ———, minister at Kirkwall; John Stewart, elder there; Mr Gilbert
Bod, minister at Holm; Alexander Somervall;
John M'Kenzie; David Monteith, servitor to my
Lord Erll of Orkney; and Gilbert Paple; with
sundry utheris; the qlk day, in presens of me,
notary publict, underwritten and witnes foirsaids, Alisoun Balfour being condempnit for
sindrie alledgit poynts of witchcraft, and lied to
the hill to the place of execution, she, in presens
of me, and witness foirsaids, declarit and tuke
upon hir saull and conscience, as she wald answer
at the day of judgement, she wes als innocent,
and wald die als innocent of ony poynt of witchcraft as ane bairne new borne; and als being
inquyrit, upon hir saull and conscience, to declair
quhat sche knew to the auld Laird of Stenhous,
and to quhat effect he gaif to hir the wax that
was in hir purs, quha then presentlie declarit, be
hir pairt of Paradyce, and as sche wald answer
to the levinge Lord, that sche knew na thing to
the auld Laird of Stenhous bot honestie; and
that his lady being subjectt to the colick, notour
to hir, willit the laird to gif heir ane peace walx,
a four zeir bygane syne, to mak ane implaister,
to be imployit be him to his ladie for remedie of
hir said diseis, and na utherwayes, as she wald
answer to the livinge God of heaven and earth;

and said than playnlie, that sche wald die with the same confession. Lykeas sche than diet constantlie therewith; and sicklyke being enquyrit and accusit be the persoun of Orphir, gif sche wald abyde be hir first deposition maid in the Castell of Kirkwall, upon the — day of December instant? quha answerit, that the tyme of hir first deposition sche was tortorit, and severall tymes in the caspieclaws, and sindrie tymes taken out of them deid, and out of all remembrance either of guid or evill; as lykewayes hir guidman being in the stokes, hir son torturit in the buits, and hir daughter put in the pilniewinks, wherwith sche and they were swa kepit and tormentit, that pairtlie to eschew ane grittar torment and pownischment; and upon promis of hir lyffe and guid deids be the said person, falslie agains hir saul and consciens sche mayd the confession, and na otherwayes; for the qlk she askit the Lord mercy and forgivenes, and constantlie deitt yratt."—*Criminal Record.*

In such diabolical times, it is not surprising that King James set himself to write his Dæmonologie, in which he sagely discovers the whole mystery of witchcraft. From its characteristic style, this tract is very amusing. He says, that the reason why women are more addicted to magick than men, "is easie, for as that sex is frailer then man is, so is it easier to be intrapped in these grosse snares of the divell, as was over-well prooved to be trew, by the serpent's deceiving of Eve at the beginning, which makes him the homelier with that sexe sensine." The persecution of unfortunate old woman by James and the clergy was somewhat relaxed after the detection of an impostor, one Margaret Atkin, who pretended to know a witch at first sight, affirming *that all of that sort had a secret mark in their eyes.*—Spottiswoode, p. 448. The mark of some was the likeness of a horse in the eye.—*Discovery of Witchcraft.* Witches and wizards, says Bodin, cannot look directly upon a man's face; nor are they able to shed tears, " threaten and torture them as ye please, while first they repent; (God not permitting them to dissemble their obstinacie in so horrible a crime,) albeit the woman-kind especially be able otherways to shed teares at every light occasion, when they will, yea, although it were dissemblingly, like the crocodiles."—*Dæmonologie,* book iii. Those who cured diseases had generally St. Catharine's wheel printed in the roof of their mouths, or in some other part about them.—*Anatomy of Melancholy,* vol. i. p. 335.

The Earl of Gowrie, whose mysterious attempt to seize upon the king at Perth, has so much puzzled historians, was exceedingly addicted to magick, as were others of his family. The word,

Tetragrammaton, written on parchment, and worn about his person, prevented the blood from flowing, even after he was dead. From the foolish conduct of the whole conspiracy, it is very probable that Gowrie laid greater stress upon such charms than a man of his reputation for abilities can easily be supposed to have done, even in that superstitious age.

This parchment was preserved long after Gowrie's death; and from what Lord Cromartie says in his Account of the Conspiracy, may still be extant;—by the way, Lord Cromartie himself might reasonably have been suspected of possessing some magical secret to secure love; for at the advanced age of seventy, he married a young and beautiful countess in her own right, a widow, wealthy, and in universal estimation. The following distich was composed on the occasion, which afforded abundant matter for waggery to the lampoon writers of the time:—

> "Thou sonsie auld carl,
>   The world hes not thy like,
> For ladies fa' in love with thee,
>   Tho' thou be ane auld tyke."

Another indignant poet exclaims,—" I swear, by all the gods, there's witchcraft in't."—*MS. Lampoons, penes me.* Lord Cromartie erected a brazen statue to the honour of his beautiful wife, with a Latin inscription, beginning thus :—

"Pulchra Venus, Pallas sapiens, et casta Diana,
Trina sub hoc uno cernitur ære Dea," &c

And dedicated his Synopsis Apocalyptica to her daughter, by a former husband, Margaret, Countess of Northesk, styling himself, "her ladyship's most obedient servant, and most affectionate father, Cromartie." This extraordinary old man, when upwards of eighty, retired, says Swift, to his estate in the Highlands, alledging that he would pass a few years there, in order to lay up money to spend in London. His son, the second earl, was in his father's lifetime tried before the Court of Justiciary for the murder of Elias Poiret, Sieur de la Roche, at Leith, and acquitted; but the death of the Frenchman seems to have been avenged by the master of Tarbet's lady, who, in the year 1693, was divorced from her husband for her gallantries with Monsieur Lavallette, a native of France, and others.—*Commissary Court Record*. It is to be observed, that this frail fair one did not carry on the family. N.B. A horn on a spirit's head signifieth that he is a count.—*Cornelius Agrippa, of Occult Philosophy.*

About the time of this conspiracy, the devil, in *propria persona*, is said to have tempted a lady near Edinburgh to murder her husband; but the fact rests only upon ballad authority   John

Kincaid of Warriston having offended his wife, by beating her, as the Criminal Record states, she contrived to strangle him, with the help of her nurse and a man-servant. The quarrel is given differently in the song :—

> " He spak a word in jest,
> Her answer wasna good ;
> He threw a plate at her face,
> Made it a' gush out o' blood."

The devil appeared shortly after, and taught her how to be avenged of this intolerable rudeness :—

> " The foul thief knotted the tether,
> She lifted his head on hie,
> The nourice drew the knot
> That gar'd Laird Warriston die."
>
> *Jamieson's Ballads.*

Birrel, in his Diary, notes,—" July 2, John Kincaid of Warristone murderit by his awin wyff, and servant-man ; (this perhaps is the *foul thief*, or devil, of the ballad,) and her nurische being also upon the conspiracy, the said gentilwoman being apprehendit, scho was tane to the Girth-Crosse, upon the 5th day of Julii, and her heid struck fra her bodie, at the Cannagait fit, quha diet very patiently ; her nurische was brunt at the same time, at 4 hours in the morning, the 5 of Junii." In the MS. Abridgment of the Justiciary Record, is this passage:—" 26 June, 1604,—William Weir, sometime servand to the Laird of Dunypace, delaytit of art and part of the cruel murder of John Kincaid of Warriston, in anno 1600. The fact of this barbarous murder is thus: Jean Livingston, spouse to the said John, having conceived a deadlie hatred towards her husband for alledged maltreatment, did send Janet Murdo, her nurse, to the said William Weir, and implored him to murder her husband, who accordingly was brought to Warriston, and about midnight they came into the room where he was lying in bed, and being awakened with the noise, called to them; whereupon the said Weir running to him, and with a severe stroke with his hand struck him on the vein-organ, (*i.e.* the flank-vein,) and thereby he fell out of his bed on the floor, whereupon Weir struck him on the bellie with his feet, and thereafter gripped him by the throat, and held him till he strangled him to death. He was sentenced to be broken alive on the row, or wheel, and be exposed thereon for 24 hours ; and thereafter the said row, with the body on it, to be placed between Leith and Warriston, till orders be given to burrie the body." " He was broken," says Birrell, " on ane cart-wheel, with ane coulter of ane pleuche, in the hand of the hangman;"—a cruel punishment, seldom to be met with in the criminal records of Scotland.

Two of the Regent Lennox's murderers, indeed, were thus executed by the Earl of Mar, "quha cawsit Bell and Calder to be publickly broken upon the row, and thus pynit to the death."—*Historie of King James the Sext,* p. 154.

Lord Fountainhall, talking of Mrs Nimmo, a daughter of Hamilton of Grange, who murdered Lord Forrester in the year 1679, says that Mrs Kincaid was of the family of Grange; but it appears that her maiden name was Livingstone. He also mentions another murderess of the same race, Mrs Bedford, whose trial occurs in the Criminal Register, 17th May, 1665. She is there styled, Margaret Hamilton, relict of Robert Bedford, Englishman, merchant at Leith, and found guilty of murder, and of an unlawful commerce with Geills Tyre, Englishman, surveyor in Leith, then prisoner in the Tolbooth of Edinburgh. "And the better to palliate the crime, under the colour of hospitality, the said Geills did take up his lodging in the said Robert his house, and was there dyeted, pretending he could not be so well accomidate elsewhere; and the said Geills did write in his books a note of the birth of these children which were his own, and of the death of such of them as deceast. And the said Geills having gone to London, she did entertain amorous correspondence with him by letters; under borrowd names, and having estranged her affection to her husband, she contrived his murder, and for that end employed a servant to buy poison; and that having failed, she did on a night bind his hands when he was in bed, upon design to murder him in his sleep; and that having also failed, so on another night, about 11 o'clock, when he was a-bed with some of his children, she did surprise and cruelly murder and strangle him; and thereafter with the cannon-bullet that she used to break her coals, did give him many deadly stroaks upon the head, and thereby killed him outright. And to palliate the murder, she resolved to bury him soon after his decease, and if the wound should be discovered, to give it out that he had it by a fall on the stair, and did take off his bloody shirt and conceal it in the cellar among the coalls, and put clean linnens upon him." Mrs Bedford, upon hearing the indictment and her former confession read, acknowledged her guilt with a flood of tears, and repeated this after the jury were sworn, and the bloody clothes and cannon-ball produced. Finally, some witnesses were called, who declared, "That they saw Bedford dead, wounded as is lybelled; and that they saw some teats of hair, and other tokens, which had been gifted to the pannel by Geills Tyre, taken out of a little coffer in her custody."— *Criminal Record.* She was condemned to be beheaded; and her lover, the presumptions of whose guilt were very strong, narrowly escaped torture, through the scruples of the Privy-council —*Sir G. Mackenzie's Works*, vol ii. p. 261.

On the 31st of July, 1603, James Reid, in Corstorphin, was convicted of sorcery, and afterwards burnt. He several times at Bannie Craigs, and on Corstorphine Muir, met the devil, (frequently in the likeness of a horse) who taught him to use south-running water as a healing charm, and enchanted flints, to the prejudice of many. Two years afterwards, Patrick Lawrie, another sorcerer, was committed to the flames on the Castle-hill of Edinburgh, for having been at sundry meetings with Sathan on Loudon-hill, where the fiend gave Patrick a hair-belt, at one end of which " appeared the similitude of four fingers and a thumb, not far different from the claws of the devil," for destroying the crops of certain farmers during the space of ten years ; for curing an *incurable* disease ; and finally, for being " ane common and notorious sorcerer, warlock, and abuser of the people."

" But, hear ye, Douce, because ye may meet me
In mony shapes to-day, where'er you spy
This browded belt, with characters, 'tis I ;
A gypsan lady, and a right beldam,
Wrought it by moonshine for me, and star light,
Upo' your granam's grave, that very night

> We earth'd her in the shades; when our dame Hecate
> Made it her gaing-night over the kirk-yard,
> When all the bark and parish tykes set at her,
> While I sat whyrland of my brazen spindle:
> At every twisted thrid my rock let fly
> Unto the sewster, who did sit me nigh,
> Under the town turn-pike, which ran each spell,
> She stitched in the work, and knit it well;
> See ye take tent to this, and ken your mother."
>
> <div align="right">Johnston's <i>Sad Shepherd</i>.</div>

In the year 1607, Isobel Grierson was burnt and her ashes scattered in the wind, after being convicted of going one night into the house of Adam Clark, in Prestonpans, in the likeness of his own cat, accompanied with a mighty rabble of cats, which, by their noise, dreadfully affrighted Adam, his wife, and maid-servant, the last of whom, the devil, in the shape of a black man, dragged up and down by the hair of the head. Grierson was also found guilty of bewitching Mr Brown of Prestonpans, by throwing an enchanted *tailzie of beef* at his door, and of causing the devil to disturb his household for the space of half-a-year, by appearing every night at his fireside in the similitude of an *infant bairn*. She herself frequently paid the family a visit in the shape of a cat, and rudely besprinkled Brown's wife, and various parts of the house, but once being called upon by name, vanished away. Brown died of a disease inflicted by her. Another wierd sister, of great note, suffered death in a few months after Isabel; this was Barbara Paterson, who was found guilty of sorcery; of anointing one John Brown, who was sick, with green salves made of herbs, and giving him drenches, and ordering him to fall down upon his knees three several times, "to ask his health at all living witches above or under the eard, in the name of Jesus." She also gave him "nine pickles of rowan-tree," (nine berries of the mountain-ash, I presume) to wear about his person. She *abused the people* with water brought from the Dow-loch, near Drumlangrig, "putting the said loch water into a stoup, and causing the patients lift it up, and say, 'I lift this stoup in the name of the Father, Son, and Holy Ghost, for the health of them for whom it was lifted;' which words were to be repeated three nine times. *Item*, she washed the patient's sark in the loch, and left it there, affirming, that if any fowl came out of the loch, the patients would recover: but if nothing came out, then they should die. *Item*, she used this charm for curing of cattle. I charm ye for arrow-shot, for eye-shot, for tongue-shot, for liver-shot, for lung-shot, for cat-shot, all the maist; in the name of the Father, Son, and Holy Ghost."

In the year 1622, Margaret Wallace was executed, principally for inflicting and curing diseases. She consulted with Christian Grahame, a witch, to remove a disorder "from Margaret Muir, a bairne; to which end they went about 12 at night to a yard, and there used their devilish charms, whereby the disease was removed from the bairne." The year after, Thomas Greave, a wizard, was burnt for curing diseases, by making sick persons pass several times through hanks of yarn, washing their shirts in south-running water, and the like. Some obscure hints in the MS. respecting the criminal's execution, would infer that the minister of the parish was as guilty as himself. In the records of the kirk-session at Eastwood, a woman is *delated* for using charms at Hallow-even. She confessed—"that, at the instigation of an old woman from Ireland, she brought in a pint of water from a well which brides and burials pass over, and dipt her shirt into it, and hung it before the fire; that she either dreamed, or else there came something and turned about the chair on which her shirt was, but she could not well see what it was." Her sentence was a rebuke before the congregation. See Burns' Poems, for an admirable detail of the charms which enliven Hallowe'en.

Isobel Young, spouse to George Smith, portioner in East Barnes, was tried for witchcraft in the year 1629. Some articles of the indictment are very singular. "*Item*, she went in a very tempestuous night, when the milne horses were scarcely able to ride it, over the water to her house, and fra her house back againe to the milne, when there was no bridge neither of stone nor timber over the water, unwet. *Item*, she destroyed the cattle of William Meslet, in great suddainty, and that by taking off her curch at the barne-door, and running about thrice within the barne widdershins. *Item*, she resett Christian Grinton, a witch, in her house, whom the pannel's husband saw one night to come out at ane hole in the roof, in the likeness of a cat, and theirafter transforme herself in her own likeness; whereupon the pannel told her husband, that it should not faire weill with him, which fell out accordingly; for next day he fell down dead at the pleuch, and was brought hame by the pannel in William Meslet's chaire. *Item*, she took a sicknesse off her husband, and laid it on his brother's son, who came to the barne, and saw the firlott running about, and the stuff popling on the floor; and he ran upon the pannell with a sword to kill her for bewitching him, and strak the lintell of the door in following; the mark whereof is to be seen yet, and that he died thereof. (See Appendix, Note 3.) *Item*, her apparition was seen in John Bryson's stable, under night, riding on ane meir, seen by David Nisbet, servand; and since, by her sorcerie, the meir cast her foal, and died. *Item,* for thir forty years, for curing of hir bestiall, she has been in use to take a quick ox, with a cat, and a great quantity of salt, and to burie the ox and cat quick with the salt, in a deep hole, as a sacrifice to the devil. (See Appendix, Note 4.) The truth of this article," continues the abridger of the Criminal Record, "was, that their bestiall being diseased of the routting evil, the pannel's husband was going to the Laird of Lee to borrow his curing-stane ; whereupon their servant, James Nisbet, told them that he had seen bestiall cured by taking a quick ox, and burying him in a pitt, and by calling the rest of the bestiall over that place; whereupon they practised it once or twice, and were not the better ; whereupon they went to the said Laird of Lee's. The ladie refused the stone, but gave flaggons of water wherein it was steiped, which giving the bestiall to drink, in their apprehension it cured them. And for using the foresaid remedy, her husband (but never the pannel) was ordained by the Presbytery of Dunbar to make satisfaction for the scandalous fact, and to divest others theirfra. It is the ordinar practice of husbandmen of the best sort, who were never suspect nor dilated of witchcraft, in many parts of the kingdom."

With regard to the stone afore mentioned, the celebrated Lee Penny, as it is commonly termed, is a small red stone, set in silver, said to have been brought from the Holy Land by Lockhart of Lee, who accompanied the Earl of Douglas when carrying King Robert the Bruce's heart to Jerusalem. Lockhart extorted it from a Paynim lady, whose husband he had taken prisoner, and who, while paying the stipulated ransom, dropt this stone from her purse. On her snatching it up with great precipitation, the wily knight divined its value, and would not relieve the infidel till the amulet was added to his price. It was long deemed a sovereign remedy for all sorts of diseases, and of late times, is said to have cured a lady of condition who was labouring under the hydrophobia. In former ages, these amulets were very common, though few have attained the celebrity of the Lee Penny. In a list of gold and jewels stolen out of the Earl of Marischall's house of Benholme (1624) by Sir Alexander Strachan of Thornton, Dame Margaret Ogilby, Countess of Marischall, his spouse, and Robert Strachan, doctor of physick, is "ane jasper stane for steiming of blood, estimat to 500 French crownes."—*Criminal Record.*

CHAPTER V.

(A.D. 1630 to A.D. 1644.)

Drummond of Auchterarder—Catherine Oswald's Indictment—Tested by the insertion of a Pin—Hattaraick Burned on the Castle Hill—The Indictment against Alie Nisbet—James Spalding Buried Alive—Many Witches on the Coasts of Fife—A notorious Warlock worried at the Stake—Executions of Barker and Lauder—The Indictment against Agnes Fynnie.

THE next unfortunate person who suffered death at Edinburgh for sorcery, was Alexander Drummond, " indweller in the Kirktown of Auchterarder, as curing thereby of frenzies, the falling evil, persons mad, distracted, or possest with fearfull apparitions, as St. Antonie's fire, the sickness *noli me tangere*, cancers, worms, glengores, with other uncouth diseases, upon many persons; also for burieng a quick ox for effectuating his sorcerie, and of pleuch-irons upon merches betwixt two lairds' lands, for curing of madness; also for having a familiar spirit attending him neir this fifty years. He confesses that such and such cures he did, but denies any incantation or charme therein. For verification of the dittay, produced his own depositiones, then the depositiones of an hundred of witnesses; whereupon, convict and burnt."

In the same year, Catharine Oswald, spouse to Robert Atchison, in Niddrie, was brought to triall for being *habite and repute* a witch, and defamed as such by Elizabeth Stevenson, *alias* Toppock, who was burnt for the crime, herself an intimate ally of the said Catharine. Toppock declared, that Oswald and she "were together in that great storm on the borrowing days, in anno 1625, on the Brae of the Saltpans;" and Alexander Hamilton, "a known warlock, even now under triall, depones, that the pannel took him one night to a den betwixt Niddrie and Edmiston, where the devill had trysted hir, where he appeared first to them like a foall, and then like a man, and appointed a new dyet at Saltcoit Muire. The fourth article of indictment beirs, that Margaret Threipland, coming to the pannel fra John Clerk, hir master, to bid hir take away hir kaill that she had growand in Straiton, because the said John had taken the milne and yard lyand thereto; she replyed, not only that she would not take away hir kaill, but also that she hoped in God that nothing should grow in that yard thereafter; according to whilk cursed *prediction*, for four years after, by hir sorcerie, neither kaill, lint, hemp, nor other graine, would grow therein, though double laboured and sowen. The fifth article beirs, that Thomas Scot, peuderer in Edinburgh, going on a morning to a mercat, met the pannel at the Pepper-milne burne, who said to him that he looked as good weill like as when Bessie Dobie was living; and parting with her, he immediately, by hir sorcerie, fell so strangely sick, that he was able to go no furder; and being carried on a coal-horse to Newbigging, he lay there till the morrow, at whilk time a wife came in to him, and told him he was forspoken. The sixth article beirs, that the pannel being offended at Adam Fairbairn and his wife, dwelling in St. Catherine's, threatened that she would be avenged upon them; conform whereto, she made their two kye run mad and rammish to deid, and also made a gentleman's bairne that they had a-fostering run wood and die. Seventh article beirs, that the pannel dwelland under William Heriot, in Lasswade, delt with the said William's master to have taine his roume over his head; but not prevailing, she removed her selfe and hir family fra that place, threatning William, and telling him that he should rew hir flitting; whereupon, immediately the time of her flitting, William's kill, full of cornes, took fire through her sorcerie. *Item*, his wife, in a frantick humour, drowned hirselfe, and one of his horse shot to deid. Eight article beirs, that John Nidrie, servitor to Patrick Heart, in the Cannogate, being 22 weeks sick of the trembling fever, came home to his mother in

Edmistoune, where the neighbours regretting his dollour, by came the pannel, and asking the cause of their lamentation, she told them and him, that if they would follow hir counsell, she would cure him soon,—which was, that he should pluck up a nettle by the root, and lay it on the hiegate side, and stale upon it three severall mornings, ere the sun rose, and sie that he were back at the house ere it rose; whilk direction he following, it cured him, which can be imputed to no virtue in the nettle, or using of it, but only to the pannell's enchantment."

Oswald's lawyers entered into very prolix and learned defences, alledging, that as the last article of accusation, " *esto* it had been so, the most it would infer would be a superstition, but no witchcraft; for what sorcerie is it to pluck up a nettle by the root, and to lay it down, and stale thereupon? specially seeing the dittay mentions no words to have been uttered by the pannell for charming the saids nettle, which tho' is used by them to be done; yea, for a recipe to the sorenesse of eyes, called the styen, its ordinar to cause them stale in such and such parts, whereby they imagine the effect will follow." Nevertheless, Catharine was found guilty, " the advocate for the instruction of the assyze producing the declaration of two witnesses, that being in the tolbuith, saw Mr John

Aird, minister, put a prin in the pannell's shoulder (where she carries the devill's mark) up to the heid, and no bluid followed theiron, nor she shrinking thereat; which was againe done in the justice-depute his own presence."

The clergy were sometimes severely punished for their zeal in the detection of witchcraft. On accusation against Margaret Wallace (burnt 1622) was, "that being conveined before the kirk session of Glasco 5 or 6 years since, by Mr Archibald Glen, minister at Carmunnock, for killing Robert Muir, his good-brother, by witchcraft she, to be revenged, laid on him ane uncouth sickness, whereof the said Mr Archibald, sweating died; to which it was answered, that in truth the said Mr Archibald died of a consumption of his lights." See Law's Memorialls, p. 127, 165.

Shortly after Catherine's execution, one of her intimates, a very celebrated wizard, was brought to the stake upon the Castle-hill. This man's names were Alexander Hunter, *alias* Hamilton *alias* Hattaraick, which last was bestowed by the devil, who first appeared to him, says Sinclair, in the form of a *medicinar;* subsequently if Alexander's confession is to be believed, he would meet him riding on a black horse, or in the shape of a *corbie,* a cat, or a dog. He gave him four shillings sterling, and a fir-tree wand teaching his slave, when desirous of a conference to strike the ground with it, and cry, "Rise up, foul thief!"—A very uncivil mode of conjuration, truly, and improbable, as dictated by Lucifer himself. However, Alexander declared that he could not get rid of him when raised in this manner, till he gave him a quick cat, dog, or other some such like thing. On one occasion, Satan chastised him severely with a cudgel. The wizard also confessed, that having conceived a deadly hatred against Elizabeth Lawson, Lady Ormiston, for having refused him *ane almous*, and called him *a custroune carl*, he, with some witches, raised the devil in Salton Wood, who, appearing like a man in gray clothes, gave him the bottom of a blue clue, and desired him to lay it at the lady's door; which he and the women having done, "the lady and her daughter were soon thereafter bereft of their naturall lyfe." Several other curious particulars respecting Hatteraick are to be found in Satan's Invisible World."

During the reign of King Henry the Fourth of France, some wizards of that country were convicted of offering to the devil such slender propitiations as a live beetle, and parings of nails.— Dr. Cotta's *Tryall of Witchcraft*.

Alie Nisbet, in Hilton, suffered death for witchcraft and adultery, (the last of which she confest) in the year 1632. It was sworn against her, that "she tooke the paines off a woman in travell, by some charmes and horrible words; amongs which thir ware some, *the bones to the fire, and the soull to the devill!* and layed them on another woman, who straight died thereof;" but Alie would not acknowledge the truth of this accusation. Two years afterwards, the king's advocate, together with Home of Ayton, and John Ramsay of Edinton, his informers, pursued Elizabeth Bathgate, spouse to Alexander Rae, maltman in Eimouth, for sorcery. "The dittay, containing 18 several articles, is as follows: 1*mo*, George Sprot, wobster in Eimouth, having claith of the pannell's, and keeping it longer than she expected, she came and violentlie took it from him, and promist to do him ane ill turne; for performing whereof, she came one morning to his house when he was fra home, and his wife lying with his bairne in the bed; she nipped the bairne in the thie till it skirled; and of which nip it never convalesced, but dwamed thereof, and died by hir sorcerie. *Item,* that the said Sprott's wife having given an egg to her bairnie that came out of the pannell's house, there did strike out a lumpe about the bigness of a goose-egg, that continued on the bairne while it died, and was occasioned by hir enchanted egg. The 2*d* article bears, that she threatened the said George Sprot that he should never get his Sunday's meat to the fore by his work; which accordingly cam to pass by hir sorcerie, he falling into extreme poverty thereafter. 3*d* article bears, that one William Donaldson having called her a witch, and she running after him to strike him for it, and he outrunning hir, she, in a fury, cryed after him, " Weill, sir, the devil be in your feit ;" whereon he straight grew impotent and cripple. 4*th*, is for laying a grievous sickness on John Gray's bairne, whereof it dyed, because they hindered you and your husband to big on the gavell of their barne. 5*th* is, that Margaret Home, spouse to Mr. John Auchterlony, came to the pannell's husband to borrow L.6 from him to help hir to buy a horse, with some more she had of hir own, which the pannel disuaded hir husband fra, yet he did it; whereon she went to the door where the horse was standing, and threatened that the horse should never do them good; conforme whereto, it died suddenlie, and swat to deid. 6*th* is, that the said Margret, coming again to borrow L.17 to buy ane ox, she opposed hir vehemently, and when hir husband, against hir will, would lend, she bewitched *the said cow* that it routed to deid; and that that night it died, there was women seen dancing on the rigging of the byre. 7*th* is, that the same Margret having borrowed more money fra the pannell's husband, which was lent altogether against hir will, and the said Margret saying that what she got of hir did no good, because it was with ill will; and having bought a horse with it, the same ran mad by the pannell's witchcraft. 8*th* is, that she was at a solemne meeting with certain witches, the devill being with them; and that she desired them to go and cast down Auchterlonie's barne, and that ane Elspeth Wilson, a witch, that was with them, desired them not to do it; whereon she went hirself and cast down the same, and some cattle was smoored. 9*th* is, that the pannell was seen to use conjurations and run withershinns in the milne of Eimouth. 10 is for laying a grievous sickness on Stevin Allan, and to have destroyed all his cattle with sorcerie. 11 is, that she was seen by two young men at 12 howers at even, (when all persons are in their beds) standing bare-legged and in hir sark valicot, at the back of hir yard, conferring with the devill, who was in gray cloaths; and when they bad hir God speid, she nor he spak not; whereon the one said to the other, "God save us, what does this woman here at this tyme of night?" the other replied, "Let hir allane, she is called not luckie." 12 is, that she caused largelie entertain one Margaret ———, a witch, apprehended at Ayton, onlie that she might not delate hir for one, who, notwithstanding, before hir conviction, declared that she was a sicker witch. 13 is for burning the milne of Eimouth, she and hir other complices witches with her. 14 is for killing David Hynd, who was watching the boats at the tyme of the herring drave on the sands of Eimouth, she and her complices; and that for fear he should have put them out. 15 is, that she had a horse-shoe layed in a secret part of the door, which the devill gave hir, assuring hir, as long as that lay there, all hir business within doors should prosper. 16 is, that William Mearnes, a notorious warlock, and who being to be tryed, put hands on himself at the devill's instigation, declared that the pannel was a witch, and that he had seen hir at several of their assemblies. 17 is, that she, with other witches, were conveyed by the devill into George Huldie's ship, which they sunk, with sundrie persons therein. 18 article is, that the pannell being confronted with sundrie other witches, they avowed in hir face that she was with them at the casting away of the forsaid ship." Wonderful to relate, this woman was acquitted!

In the year 1638, one James Spalding, residing in Dalkeith, was hanged for the murder of William Saidler, "by straiking him throw the temples with a whinger on the Hie striet of Dalkeith, and for invaiding and wounding Mr. Robert Burnet, advocat."—*Criminal Record.*

This is the Spalding of whom Sinclair tells so wonderful a story in his Satan's Invisible world. After having in vain begged mercy from Lord Traquair, he was condemned to be hanged, which seems to have extremely wounded his pride, as he exclaimed, "Oh, must I die like a dog! Why was I not sentenced to loose my head?" And on the scaffold he prayed,— "Lord, let this soul of mine never depart from this body till it be reconciled with thee." Accordingly, it was found impossible to strangle him, and he was buried alive, making "such a rumbling and tumbling in his grave, that the very earth was raised, and the mules were so heaved up that they could hardly keep them down. After this, his house at the east end of the town was frequented with a ghost." In the same year, "Thomas Crombie, sometyme porter and servand to ane noble and mychty earle, John Earle of Traquaire, his majesty's great thesaurer of Scotland, was pursued at the instance of the king's advocate, for hamesucken, demembration, and other crymes, *ut infra*. The said Thomas, for his lewdnesse, being shute out of my Lord Traquaire's service, and threatened never to be seen there again, he, in revenge theirof, knowing that my lord was at court in England, came to the Castle of Dalkeith, where he knew was my Ladie Traquaire and hir children; and, by way of hamesucken, with a sword, whinger, and other weapons, entered within the court of the said palace, and hearing that the ladie was in the garden, rushed therein, and came towards hir with his drawn sword, uttering thir words,—' Now I shall have amends of thee,' and then strak at hir with intention to kill, which certainly he would have done, had not a servant of the ladie's there besyde come betwixt hir and it, and which lighted on the said Mr John Lawson his shoulder, and wounded him sore, whereon they fell a strugling; during which tyme the ladie made hir escape to the house, and in which the said Thomas, with the whinger, gave him again two great wounds, and left him sounding in his blood, and came seiking the ladie again, where, falling on another servant, he most cruelie mutilat him of his thumb. He was convict, and sentenced to be hanged at Dalkeith."—*Justiciary Record.* See also Baillie's Letters.

" About this time many witches are taken in Anstruther, Dysart, Culros, St. Andrews, and other parts on the coast side of Fife. They made strange confessions, and were burnt to the death." —Spalding's *History*, vol. ii. p. 102. One John Brugh, " a notorious warlock in the parachin of Fossoquhy, by the space of 36 years," was *worried at a stake and brunt*, 1643. The same year, Janet Barker, and Margaret Lauder, "indwellers and servands in Edinburgh, were convicted of witchcraft. They confessed that one Janet Cranstone, a notorious witch, introduced them to the devil, who promised, that they should be as trimlie cled as the best servands in Edinburgh." From some ridiculous circumstances in their confessions, I am induced to think that the witches had read the story of Europa. Barker acknowledged having the devil's mark between her shoulders, which was found; and a pin being thrust therein, it remained for an hour unperceived by the paunell. The year after these executions, Agnes Fynnie, dwelling at the Potterrow Port of Edinburgh, was prosecuted for witchcraft. "Her dittay is as follows: That whereas by the 18th chap. of Deuteronomy, and 20th of Leviticus, and 73d act of the ninth parliament of Q. Marie, all sorcerie is prohibit; yet the said Agnes hes committed the crymes following: 1st article, that having threatened Mr. William Fairlie's son to send him halting home, because in a nickname, going by her door, he called hir *Annie Winnie*, he within 24 howers after lost the power of his left syde by hir witchcraft, and languished in so incurable a disease, that the whole physicians called it supernaturall, and the haill substance of his bodie ran out at his cute; and the boy laid the wholle wyte of his death constantlie upon the pannell: 2d article is, that she laid upon Beatrix Nisbet a fearfull disease, so that she lost *the power of her tongue!* because she paying the said Agnes two dollars owing hir by hir father, would not give hir annual rent therefor: The 3d is, that she laid a grievous sickness upon Jonet Grinton, whom ye threatened that she should never eat more in this world, because she had brought again two herring she had bought from you, they not being caller, and sought back hir 8 pennies, and of which she died, without eating or drinking, conforme to your threatening: The 4th is, that ye came in to visit John Buchannan's bairne, being sick of a palsie, and bad the father and mother go ben the house a whylle, and pray to God for him; and in the mean whylle ye staid with him, and when they returned, they fand him violently sick that he could neither stirr hand nor foot, and that by your devilrie; and fand on his right buttock, about the bridth of one's loofe, the same so sore as if a collope had been tain out of it; and he died within 8 days, in great dolour: The 5th is, that falling a scolding with Bessie Currie, the said bairne's mother, about the changing of a sixpence which ye alledged to be ill, ye, in great rage, threttned that ye should gar the devill tack a bite of hir: The 6th is, that ye laid a grievous sickness on hir husband, Jo. Buchannan, that he

brant a wholle night as if he had been in a
fyre, for taking his wife Bessie Currie's part
against you, and boasting to cast you over the
stair, and calling you a witch; whereon ye
thretned him to make him repent his speeches;
and for taking the same off him, he coming
the next day and drinking a pint of aill with
you, and telling you that if you tormented
him so another night, he should make all the
toun heir tell of it; whereon he was weill. The
7th is, that the said John being offended at
you because ye would not thrist his wife a
12-pennie caik, ye bad him go his way, and as
he had begun with witches, so he should end;
after which threatening, he streight contracted
a long and grievous sicknesse, whereof he was
lyke to melt away in sweiting. The 8th is,
that in your scolding with Euphame Kincaid,
ye calling hir a drunkard, and she calling you
a witch, ye replied, 'That if ye was a witch,
she and hir's should have better cause to call
ye so;' accordingly a gret jist fell on the said
Euphame's daughter's leg, being playing near
your house, and crushed the same, and that by
your sorcery. The 9th is, that ye ending a compt
with Isobell Atchesone, and because ye could
not get all your unreasonable demands, ye bad
the devill ride about the toune with hir and
hir's; whereupon the nixt day she brak hir

leg by ane fall from a horse, and ye came and saw hir, and said, " Sie that ye say not that I have bewitched you, as other neighbours say.' The 10*th* is, that Robert Wat, deacon of the cordiners, having fyned Robert Pursell, your sone-in-law, for a riot, ye came where he and the rest of the craft ware conveined, and cursed them most outragiously, whereon Robert Wat broke the cap upon your head (See Appendix, Note 5); since which tyme he fell away in his worldly means, till long after, he being in your good-son's house, where ye likeways was, ye asked, 'if he remembered since he broke the cap on your head? and that he had never thriven since, nor should, till you had amends of him;' whereon he being reconciled with you, he prospered in his worldly estate as before. The 11*th* is, the laying on of a grievous sickness on Christian Harlaw, for sending back a plack's worth of salt which ye had sent hir, it being too little; ye having threatened hir that it should be the dearest salt ever she saw with her eyes, and then, at hir entreaty, ye came to her house, and she became presentlie weill; whereon Christian said, 'that if ought ailled hir thereafter, she should wyt you.' The 12*th* is, that Christian Sympsone being owing you some money, and because she craved only eight dayes delay to pay it, ye threatened, in great rage, 'that she should have a sore heart or that day eight dayes;' according whereto, the said Christian's husband broke his leg within the said eight dayes. The 13*th* is, that John Robieson having called you a witch, you, in malice, laid a flux on him by your sorcerie. The 14*th* is, for appearing to John Cockburne in the night, when both doors and windows were fast closed, and terrifieng him in his sleep, because he had discorded with your daughter the day before. The 15*th* is, for causing all William Smith's means evanish, to the intent he might never be able to relieve some cloaths he had panded besyde you, worth an 100lb. for 14 merks Scots onlie. The 16*th* is, for onlaying a grievous sicknesse on Janet Walker, lying in childbed; and then ye being sent for, and the said Janet's sister begging her health at you for God's sake, ye assented, and she recovered of hir sicknesse presently by your sorcerie. The 17*th* is, that ye being disappointed of having Alexander Johnstone's bairne's name, ye, in a great rage and anger, told him, 'that it should be telling him 40lb. betwixt and that tyme twelfmonth, that he had given you his bairne's name;' whereon he tooke a strange sickness and languished long; and at length, by persuasive of neighbours, he came to your house, and after he had eaten and drunken with you, ye with your sorcerie made him wholle. *Item* the child whose name ye got not was past eleven years ere she could go. The 18*th* is, that ye having fallin in a contraversie with Margaret Williamsone, ye most outrageously wished the devill to blow hir blind; after which, she, by your sorcerie, took a grievous sicknesse, wherof she went blind. The 19*th* is, for laying a madness on Andrew Wilson, conforme to your threatening, wishing the devill to ryve the soul out of him, (which words, the tyme of his frenezie, ware ever in his mouth) and that because he had fallen in a brauling with your daughter. *Item*, for taking off it. The 20*th* article is a generall, for beiring companie with the devill these 28 years bypast; for consulting with him for laying on and taking off diseases, als weill on men as women and' bestiall, which is nottourly known. *Item*, it is confest by hirself, that she has been commonlie called a rank witch these many years bygane, and has been sua diffamed, repute, and halden."

The unhappy culprit's defences were long and able. Among other proofs of her innocence, it was alleged, that though many witches had been burnt at Leith and Edinburgh for these twenty years past, she was never accused by any of them; and that when her house was searched by Bailie John Ellies, "there was neither pictur, toad, nor any such thing found therein, which ever any witch in the world was used to practize." Nevertheless, she was condemned to be worried at a stake, and then burnt to ashes.

CHAPTER VI.
(A.D. 1645 to A.D. 1669.)

The Death of Charles I. and Civil War Predicted—Hidden Treasure supposed to be guarded by Spirits—Davy Ramsay, Clockmaker—The Marquis of Montrose influenced—Strange Sights at General Leshley's House—Precognition of Approaching Death—The Earl of Holland's Death—Two "Remarkables"—Numerous Witch Burnings on the Restoration of Charles II.—The Cases of Margaret Bryson, Isabel Ramsay, and Margaret Hutcheson.

WHILST these unhallowed practises went on in a more private circle, the powers of darkness were busy with the greatest personages in the three kingdoms; but this black mass of wickedness came to a point before Whitehall, where a king was publicly murdered by a masked executioner, a lively emblem of that party which brought him to the block. "It is said that some lions in the tower died at the smell of a handkerchief dipt in the blood of King Charles the First."—*Wonders of Nature,* by W. Turner, 1697. Charles's fate, if we are to believe Lilly, had been predicted to his mother, Queen Anne, by one English, or Inglis, a Scotsman, as that of

Buckingham was foretold by a Highland seer, who said,—"Pish, he will come to nothing; I see a dagger in his breast."—Aubrey's *Miscellanies*, p. 275. The miseries of the civil war was also foreshown by prodigies of a monster seen in the river Don; the disappearance of sea-gulls from the lakes near Aberdeen; loud tucking of drums heard in Mar, and in a seaman's house at Peterhead, where trumpets, bagpipes, and tolling of bells, gave additional horror to the sound.—Spalding's *History*.

One of the ridiculous pursuits of that time was a search after hidden treasure, supposed to be guarded by spirits, with all the elemental powers at their command. In the year 1634, Davy Ramsay, his majesty's clockmaker, made an attempt to discover a precious deposit supposed to be concealed in the cloister of Westminster Abbey, but a violent storm of wind put a stop to his operations.—Lilly's *Life*, p. 47. This Ramsay, according to Osborne, in his Traditional Memorials, used to deliver money and watches, to be recompensed with profit, when King James should sit on the Pope's chair at Rome, so near did he apprehend (by astrology, doubtless,) the downfall of the papal power. His son wrote several books on astrological subjects, of which his *Astrologia Restaurata* is very entertaining. In the preface, he says that his father was of an ancient Scottish family, viz. of Eightherhouse (Auchterhouse) "which hath flourished in great glory for 1500 years, till these latter days;" and derives the clan from Egypt, (it is wonderful that the idea of gypsies did not startle him) where the word Ramsay signifies joy and delight. But he is extremely indignant that the world should call his father "no better than a watchmaker," asserting that he was in fact page of the bedchamber, groom of the privy-chamber, and *keeper of all his majesties clocks and watches.* "Now, how this," quoth he to the reader, "should prove him a watchmaker, and no other, more than the late Earles of Pembroke, ordinary chamberlains, because they bore this office in the king's house, do thou judge." It may be here observed, that even the sagacious inventor of the logarithms participated in the folly of his majesty's watchmaker, or keeper, in searching after hidden treasures. See a curious proof of this in Wood's Peerage of Scotland. The same Sir Archibald Napier, from his superior knowledge and retired habits, was deemed a wizard by the vulgar; and this honour to his country was supposed to entertain a familiar in the shape of a large black cock, from which he received advice in his scientific studies, and responses as to futurity.

In King Charles the First's reign, a certain fair

Scottish countess is said to have eloped with a band of gypies, owing to the *glamour* exercised by their leader. The ballad composed on this subject is well known; but if chronology were not against it, I should believe that a poem by Captain Alexander Montgomery, author of the Cherrie and Slae, had also been written on the same event. It is termed, "A Ladyis Lamentation," and begins thus :—

"Quhom suld I warie but my wicked weard,
Quha span my thriftles thraward fatall threed!
I wes but skantlie entrit in this eard,
Nor had offendit quhill I felt hir feed,
In hir unhappy hands sho held my heid,
And straikit bakward woodershins my hair,
Syne prophecyed I sould aspyre and speid ;
Quhilk double sentence was baith suith and sair,
For I wes matchit with my match and mair,
No worldly woman never wes so weill ;
I wes accountit countess, but compair,
Quhill fickle Fortune whirld me from her wheel,
Rank and renoun in little roum sho rang'd,
And Lady Lucrece in a Cresseid chang'd," &c.

The Marquis of Montrose is said to have been confident of success in his last unfortunate expedition, through some fallacious prophecies, to the belief of which he was greatly addicted, assuring him that he should conquer Scotland, and from thence conduct an army to settle the king in all his dominions—Echard's *History*. At this hero's birth, his mother consulted with witches, and it was predicted that he would trouble all Scotland. "He is said also," continues the author of the Staggering State, "to have eaten a toad whilst he was a sucking child." In maturer life, he did worse,—he swallowed the Covenant. The following curious detail respecting the apparition of a rival general, whose military fame was obscured by abominable acts of cruelty, is extracted from a Diurnal of the time:—"*Edinburgh, 4th January,* 1649, There was lately, upon a Lord's day, a very strange sight at St. Johnston's, at which town Lieutenant-General David Leshley hath an house, himself being then at church, where two of his men being at home, they saw (as they thought) an ensign fastened like a standard upon the tower of his house, which caused them to go up, having not known of any such thing put there. When they came up there, as they say, they being on the top of the tower, looked upon it, and there seemed to be the picture of their master, Lieut.-General David L. riding upon his charging horse, in his buffe coat, and in that posture in which he used to march, and upon it also the motto of his own colours. One of the men going near to the flagge to hold it in his hand, or touch it, before he did touch it, the staffe, and colour, and all fell down into the midst of the garden, whether they went down to take it up again. When they came into the garden, and thought to have found it there, it was gone; and none knows any thing more of it, only what these two thus saw. They went presently to the church to tell their master what they had seen, and what befell them, and to ask him about it, and whether he knew of any such ensign set up there. This newes hath much amased them hereabouts; some making a good construction of it to Scotland, others bad, and good to England. Some think that the men were seduced by an evil spirit, and some think they are very knaves."

Sir Richard Napier, descended from the Merchiston family, and a doctor of medicine in London, during the reign of King Charles I. saw his own apparition, as dead, and laid out upon a bed, a little while previous to his death. This is mentioned by Aubrey, who also relates, that "the beautiful Lady Diana Rich, daughter to the Earl of Holland, as she was walking in her father's garden at Kenington, to take the fresh air before dinner, about eleven o'clock, being then very well, met with her own apparition, habit, and every thing, as in a looking-glass.

About a month after, she died of the small-pox ; and it is said that her sister, the Lady Isabella Thynne, saw the like of herself also, before she died. (See Appendix; Note 6.) This account I had from a person of honour." A third daughter of Lord Holland was the wife of the first Earl of Breadalbane ; and it has been recorded that she also, not long after her marriage, had some such warning of her approaching dissolution.

Wodrow, in his History of the Sufferings of the Church of Scotland, mentions two *remarkables*, as he terms them, which took place in Scotland on the restoratian of King Charles, and the removal of the English troops : " When the English subdued Scotland, the swans which were in the loch on the north side of Linlithgow, left it, and, as it was then termed, took banishment on them ; but last year, or the beginning of this, they came back upon the king's return. And upon the Citadell of Perth, where the arms of the Commonwealth had been put up, in May last year, a thistle grew out of the wall near the place, and quite overspread them, which was much observed, and our old Scotch motto, *Nemo me impune lacessit*. Both these may be, without anything extraordinary, accounted for ; but they were matter of remark and talk, it may be, more than they deserved."

Whatever satisfaction the return of King

Charles the Second might afford to the younger females in his dominions, it certainly brought nothing, save torture and destruction, to the unfortunate old women, or witches of Scotland, against whom, immediately on the restoration, innumerable warrants were issued forth; and for some years the Castlehill of Edinburgh, and the heights in the vicinity, blazed with the dry carcases of those miserable victims; nor was this persecution confined to Mid Lothian, but widely extended over the northern counties, where ignorant justices of the peace, abetted by foolish clergymen, doomed almost every old woman *dilated*, as it was called, by some of her spiteful neighbours, to the torture and the stake. Sir George Mackenzie affirms, that he knew a witch burnt "because the lady was jealous of her with her husband." Of the trials for witchcraft in Edinburgh after the restoration, a few extracts are subjoined.

August 1661, Margaret Bryson, and several other witches, were condemned and executed. "Bryson's case," says the abridger of the Criminal Record, "I note down to be a warning against passion and imprecations; she having fallen out with her husband for selling her cow, she went out in a passion to the door of her house in the night time, and there did imprecat that God or the devill might take her from her husband; after which, immediately the devill appeared to her, and threatened to take her, soul and body, if she entered not into his service; whereupon immediately she covenanted with him, and renunced her baptism." In the case of Isabel Ramsay, it appeared "that she conversed with the devil, and received a sixpence from him; the devil saying that God bad him give her that; and he asked, how the minister did? She confessed that she received a dollar from the devil, which thereafter she found to be a sklait-stone. Against Margaret Hutcheson it is lybelled, that she threatened John Boost for calling her a witch; and within a few days thereafter, by throwing a piece of raw flesh into his house, which was burnt in the fire, (after dogs and catts had refused to eat it) a disease seized on his cat, which made her to fight and sweat to death; that she threatened John Bell for contending with her husband, and immediately thereafter, three cats entered to his house, which were like to devour them, whereupon two of his children died, and his wife contracted a long disease; that she appeared several nights at midnight, combing her head at the fireside, doors being shut, and affrighted his wife; and the last of these nights, by her touching the wife's pap, when her child was sucking, the child died.

In the City Records of Edinburgh, after a gift

of escheat, granted by the council to the baron
bailie of Canongate, of all heritable and moveable goods belonging to the witches thereof,
(17th July, 1661) follows a Report made by
William Johnstone, baron bailie of Canongate,
concerning Barbara Mylne, whom Janet Allen,
burnt for witchcraft, "did once see come in at
the Water-gate in likeness of a catt, and did
change her garment under her awen staire, and
went into her house." This, and the other flying
reports, caused the bailie to think it proper to
detain the said Barbara in prison till he
acquainted the council. The gift of escheat,
no doubt, had its proper weight with him; but
he is desired to take caution for her appearance,
and to liberate her till some course be taken for
further examination.

Another witch, Janet Cock, was accused of
making many persons of both sexes run mad.
"*Item*, she killed a child of William Scott's,
fostered by Helen Turnbull, having predicted the
same by these words, *that she* (Helen) *should get
her leave from her master, and a lash* ——; she
having conceived hatred against William Mitchell
for smiting her, said, she would see him hanged,
and make a shameful end; and accordingly he
was hanged at Dalkeith. She kept company
with the devil, and came with him and several
of his associates to Elizabeth Pringle's house,

when the doors of the house were close, and wrestled to get from her the child in her arms. She bewitched William Scott's horse, and turned him furious; and a country man, present for the time, having caused Scott to take off the horse shoes, and put them in the fire, telling him, that the first person who should come in after the shoes should be taken hot out of the fire, would be the witch; immediately the pannel came in, who was never in the house before, and without any business. In anno 1661, she predicted and foretold that a whirlwind should arise, and take away Christian Wilson, a suspected witch, in her transport from Dalkeith to Niddrie, where she was to be confronted with other persons, which accordingly fell out." To this last last article her lawyer, Mr. Andrew Birnie, answered, that she only said, would it not be good sport if a wind would come and take away the person libelled from those who transported her? From some passages of the trial, it appears that Cock used those applications of newly killed animals to sick persons, once so extensively practised. "Margaret Brunton, a confessing witch, did declare in face of the pannel, that about 16 years ago, she being in the house of James Steel in Dalkeith, visiting a sick child, she saw the pannel, and Jean Dickson, another witch, lying over the child and whispering to one another, and they commanded Margaret Brunton to go from them; and that after Janet and the dog of the house had been some time together in a close room, the door being open, the dog rushed out, and Janet was found with another woman, and a plate of blood standing beside them; and the dog was found dead within the house, its head amissing, and the child immediately recovered." The dog's head had been applied to the child. In that curious book, The Poor Man's Physician, or the Receits of the famous John Moncrief of Tippermalloch, the reader will find many such barbarous prescriptions, together with numberless other most beastly and fatal nostrums, with which our charitable grandmothers were daily wont to poison their own family, and half the parish besides.

The Privy Council, in the year 1662, granted a commission to several gentlemen for trial of some witches in the parish of Innerkip, who had made ingenuous confessions. Among which the following extraordinary document, printed from the MS., obligingly communicated to me by Michael Stewart Nicolson, Esq., is well worthy of preservation.

"The Confession of Marie Lamont, a young Woman of the adge of Eighteen Yeares, dwelling in the parish of Innerkip, who willinglie offered herself to Tryell on the 4th of March, 1662.

"1. She cam and offered herself willingly to the tryell, saying, that God moved her heart to confess, because she had lived long in the devil's service. 2. She confessed most ingenuously, that fyve years since, Kattrein Scot, in Mudiestean, within the parochin of Innerkip, learned her to take kyes milk, biding her goe owt in mistie mornings, and take with her a harrie tedder, and draw it over the mouth of a mug, saying, 'In God's name, God send us milk, God send it, and meikle of it.' By this meanes shee and the said Kattrein gat much of their neighbour's milk, and made butter and cheise thereof. (For more particulars concerning this charm, see Kirk's Secret Commonwealth, p. 5.) 3. She confessed that two yeares and ane half since, the devill came to the said Kattrein Scott's house, in the midst of the night, wher wer present with them, Margret M'Kenzie in Greinok, Janet Scot in Gorrok, herself, and several others; the devill was in the likeness of a meikle black man, and sung to them, and they dancit; he gave them wyn to drink, and wheat bread to eat, and they warr all very mirrie. She confesses, at that meiting the said Kettie Scott made her first acquaintance with the devill, and caused her to drink to him, and shak hands with him. 4. She confesses, that at that tyme the devill bad her betak herself to his service, and it sould be weel with her, and bad her forsak her baptizme, which shee did, delyvering herself wholly to him, by putting her one hand on the crown of her head, and the other hand to the sole of her fott, and giving all betwixt these two into him. 5. She confessed, that at that tyme he gave her name, and called her *Clowts*, and bad her call him *Serpent*, when she desired to speak with him. 6. Shee confessed, that at that sam tym the devill nipit her upon the right syd, qlk was very painful for a tym, but yairefter he straikit it with his hand, and healed it; this she confesses to be his mark." The seventh article regards her criminal intercourse with Sathan as to gallantry, which she first confessed, and then denied. "8. She confesses that she was at a meitting in the Bridylinne, with Jean King, Kettie Scot, Margrat M'Kenzie, and several others, where the devill was with them in the likeness of a brown dog. The end of their meitting was to raise stormie weather to hinder boats from the killing fishing; and shee confessed that shee, Kettie Scot, and Margrat Holm, cam to Allan Orr's house in the likeness of kats, and followed his wif into the chalmer, where they took a herring owt of a barrell, and having taken a byt off it, they left it behind them; the qlk herring the said Allan his wif did eat, and yairefter taking heavy disease, died. The quarrel was, because the said Allan had put Margrat Holm out of the houss wher shee was dwelling, whereupon shee threitened in wrath, that he and his wif sould not be long together. This agrees with the tent article of Kettie Scot's confession. 10. Shee confessed, that shee, Kettie Scot, Margrat M'Kenzie, and severall others, went out to the sea betwixt and the land of Arran, to doe skaith to boats and ships that sould com alongs. They caused the storme to increase greatly, and mieting with Colin Campbell's ship, did rive the sailles from her. Shee confesses, that in that voyadge shee was so oversett with ill weather that shee took the fever soon yairefter, and did bleed much. This agrees with the 12th artickle of Kettie Scot's confession. 11. Shee confessed, that when shee had been at a mietting sine Zowle last, with other witches, in the night, the devill convoyed her home in the dawing; and when shee was com near the hous wherein shee was a servant, her master saw a waff of him as he went away from hir. 12. She confessed, that shee knew some witches caried meikle ill will at Blackhall, younger, and Mr John Hamilton, and would fain give them ane ill cast if they could; therefor, about five weeks sine, Jean King, Kettie Scot, Jonet Holm, herself, and severall others, met together in the night, at the back gate of Ardgowand, where the devill was with them in the likeness of a black man, with cloven featt, and directed some of them to fetch wyt sand from the shore, and cast it about the gates of Ardgowand, and about the minister's house; but shee sayes, when they war about that business, the devil turned them in likeness of kats, by shaking his hands above their heads. She confesses alsoe, that in that business some were cheifs and ringleaders, others was bot followers. This agrees with the 11th article of Kettie Scot's confession. 13. Shee confessed alsoe, that shee was with Katie Scot, Margrat M'Kenzie, and others, at a meitting at Kempoch, where they intendit to cast the longston into the sea, thereby to destroy boats and shipes, wher they danced, and the devil kissed them when they went away. These artickles were confessed by the said Marie Lamont, at Innerkip, before us, undersubscribers Archibald Stewart, fiare of Blackhall; J. Hamilton, minister at Innerkip," &c.

One of the most remarkable circumstances in this curious confession, is that of the devil's singing, his voice being represented by witches as hollow and *goustie*, and the music with which he regaled them generally instrumental. In Satan's Invisible World, however, there is a story (attested by a reverend minister) of a piper to whom the devil, "at a ball of dancing," taught an obscene song, "to sing and play as it were this night, and ere two days passed, all the lads and lasses of the town were lilting it through the streets. It were an abomination," adds Sinclair, "to rehearse it." In truth the Scottish minstrels of every description were vulgarly supposed, during the prevalence of the Covenant, to be under the peculiar care and protection of the devil. Nay, even the Reverend Mr. Kirk, author of the Secret Commonwealth, would insinuate, that in Ireland and in the north of Scotland a sensibility to the charms of music, so as to occasion dancing, proceeds from diabolic influence. "Irish-men," says he, "our northern Scotish, and our Athole men, are so much addicted to, and delighted with harps and musick, as if, like King Saul, they were possessed with a forrein spirit; only with this difference, that musick did put Saul's play-fellow asleep, but roused and awaked our men, vanquishing their own spirits at pleasure, as if they were impotent of its powers, and unable to command it; for wee have seen some poor beggars of them chattering their teeth for cold, that how soon they saw the fire, and heard the harp, leap thorow the house like goats and satyrs."

But if the bagpipe could inspirit the godly to fight for the good old cause, it was hallowed forthwith. Lord Lothian, writing to Lord Ancram from the Scottish army at Newcastle, 18th February, 1641, says,—"I cannot out of our armie furnish yow with a sober fidler; there is a fellow here plays exceeding well, but he is intollerably given to drink; nor have we many of these people. Our armie hes few or none that carie not armes. We are sadder and graver than ordinarie soldiers, only we are well provided of pypers; I have one for every company in my regiment, and I think they are as good as drummers." The bagpipe itself seems to have been a favourite instrument with the devil :—At the witch meeting in Alloway kirk,

"He screw'd the pipes and gart them skirl,
Till roof and rafters a' did dirle."

Burns' *Tam o' Shanter*.

And there was a legend long current in Glasgow, that about an hundred years ago, as a citizen was passing at midnight through the churchyard which surrounds the Cathedral, he saw a neighbour of his own, lately buried, rise out of his grave, and dance a jig with the devil, who played the air, called, "Whistle o'er the lave o't," upon the bagpipe, which struck the whole city with so much horror, that the town-drummer forbid any one to play, sing, or whistle the nefarious tune in question.

Patrick Walker, in his Vindication of Mr. Cameron, enveighs thus eloquently against dancing to bagpipes and fiddles:—" I have often wondered thorow my life, how any who ever knew what it was to bow a knee in earnest to pray, durst crook a hough to fyke and fling at pipers' and fidlers' springs. I bless the Lord that ordered my lot so in my dancing days, that made the fear of the bloody rope and bullets to my neck and head, the pain of boots, thumbikins, and irons, cold and hunger, wetness and weariness, to stop the lightness of my head, and the wantonness of my feet. What the never-to-be-forgotten man of God, John Knox, said to Queen Mary, when she gave him that sharp challenge, which would strike our mean-spirited, tongue-tacked ministers dumb, for his giving publick faithful warning of the danger of church and nation, through her marrying *the dauphine of France*, (he should have said Lord Darnley) when he left her bubbling and greeting, and came to an outer court where her Lady Maries were fyking and dancing, he said,—' O brave ladies, a brave world if it would last, and heaven at the hinderend; but fy upon the knave Death, that will seize upon these bodies of yours;—and where will your fidling and flinging be then?'

Dancing being such a common evil, especially among young professors, has caused me to insist the more upon it, especially that foolish spring, the Cameronian march." Mrs. Macbirnie, a pious widow of Dumfries, who was sent to Dunnotter Castle for whiggery, and wrote an account of her tribulations, complains grievously of the Fife militia, appointed to guard her and other old women, because they called them old witches, wishing the devil to take them and their religion, and of "the pipers, who, by the way, derided them with their foolish songs."—*Wodrow's MS.*

The most remarkable scene of witchcraft during the reign of King Charles the Second, was acted in Renfrewshire, where Sir George Maxwell of Pollock died, as it was supposed, from the malice of some haggs and one wizard. A full account of this strange affair will be found in the Memorialls, to which the following letter from the Reverend Mr. Robert Knox, to the Rev. Mr. Wyllie, is a proper addition. It is printed from the original, one passage only being omitted, as too specific regarding the intimacy of the devil with the youngest witch, Annabel Stewart:—

Cavers, Feb. 27, 77.

My dear Friend,
Yours of Feb. 2 (which I received the 24) hath

mightily convinced me (I say not that theer are witches, for it is a good tyme since I was past doubting of yt truth) that these persones who are apprehended upon that score by the Laird of Pollock's friends, and who, probably, ere this, have suffered upon earth for their crimes, are really such; the finding of the effigies; the observed influence the withdrawing the pines from them had upon the gentilman, albeit he was not acquainted therewith; (as I am glad to finde you intimate in your last that Housle did, for I suppose you insinuat that at Housle's returne from J. Stewart's house, he enquired how Pollock found himself, befor he knew anything of what he had done,) together with the confession obtained without tortur, and their agrieng in confession about the last effigies making; which confessions, I presume, were received apart, do free me of any solid or rational objection to the contrair; neither in all their confessions (which I hugg thee, dear Robin, for sending to me) doe I observe any thing that those who believe the existence of devils can imagine them uncapable to perform; their is not theirin the taking different shape from what nature gave them, and flying therein through the air, or the lyke prodigious account of succubi and incubi divels, which other witches, with many other odd stories, do confesse, and which, in my opinion, are possible. And indeed I judge Dumby (*i.e.* Janet Douglas,) the greatest prodigy in the whole business, and would gladly be satisfied of her birth and education. I should had good thoughts of her, if it had not been her making take blood of the criminalls; but I observe, from your information, her age, her deafness and dumbness, which make it improbable she had that charme from observation and experience. I am convinced this came the same way to her that the rest of her extraordinar sagacity came, which, for all this, I dare not impute positively to an evil cause. You know that pairte of the Christian church, which is so considerable, as to assume to itself the title of Catholick, holds the history of Tobiah, where there is an action, (which, in my judgement,) hath more resemblance to a charme than yet this hath, enjoined and taught by an angel, cannonical scripture—(See Appendix, note 7). It is our ignorance of the power of any naturall agent that makes us impute y effects to evil spirits, which we fancy they produce upon our paying them our hommage, by making use of some charme which they have taught. This made the powder of sympathy, when first it was used in Europe, ill lookt on, and many divers into naturall philosophy, be deemed magicianes. This taking of blood from the witch above the breath, may possibly have a naturall ability to restraine her from further injuring the person that gave it passage, or upon whose score it was taken, and this possibly by creating in her a pannick feare (which you know a guilty conscience is very susceptible of) of them. And now, since I have entred a field of possibilities, where you know there is roome enough to roame in, I'le pass on a litle further, and spend the remnant of this paper on my toure. Possibly, then, Mrs. Dumby hath some correspondence with some of Mr. Dryden's changelings of heaven, his aërial spirites, which have taught her all this skill, and which probably, are intimately acquaint with the power of natur, and have easy access to all our litle business here below, and are able to give their favourites clear information thereof. They are they whom the vulgar call white deviles, which possibly have neither so much power nor malice as the black ones have, which served our great grandfathers under the names of Brouny, and Robin Goodfellow, and, to this day, make dayly service to severals in quality of familiars; and ir all tales be trew, they have been observed to be effrayed at the presence of a black spirit. I have heard a story of a lady in our west marches 'twixt Ingland and us, who had one whom she named Ethert, which alwais appeared to her, and was ever in her presence when she was alone, in the shape of a litle old fellow. She was one night

passing a large muire, with no attendants but
Ethert running by her, when there appeared a
big unshapely spirit, at which Ethert jumpt
on horseback behind my lady, and all the
tyme that the black one attended them, Ethert
clasped his armes about my lady, and shivered
and trembled, and appeared to be in a greater
fear by far than my lady herself—(See Appendix,
note 8). But my serious thoughts of the matter
is, that this discovery may be of good weight
with others, to prove the existence of a power
able to free us from their malice, and infinitly
good, saving us many tymes when we little dreed
danger from them. To whose power, that you
and I may be entirely devoted, is the most serious
desire of your own

Ro. Knox.

For Mr Robert Wyllie, at Ochiltree, to be delivered to Walter
   Cunningham, bookseller, hard
   by the Cross, on the south syde
   of the streete, Edinburgh.

I know assuredly, that Janet Douglas, that
was first a dumbie, yet spoke thereafter, who had
given many responses by signs and words, and
foretold many future events, being examined by
Mr. Gray, one of the ministers of the city of
Glasgow, denyed any explicit or implicit paction;

and declared freely, that the answers of the questions proposed to her were represented by a vision, and lively images representing the persons concerned, and acting the thing, before her eyes. This Master Gray exchanged several discourses in writ with Sir James Turner, concerning her."—*A Discourse of the Second Sight, by the Rev. Mr. John Frazer, Minister of Teree and Coll, and Dean of the Isles.*

CHAPTER VII.
(A.D. 1668 to A.D. 1683.)

Strange Apparitions in the Covenanting Times—At Rutherglen—At Craigmad—At Darmead—Curious Beliefs regarding the Royalists on the part of the Covenanters—The Ghost of Spedlin's Castle—" The Laying of a Gaist"—Wonderful Revelations at Monzie—A Witch Burned at Crieff—Graves Unaccountably Prepared.

PATRICK WALKER, writing of the persecution of fanatics during the reign of Charles the Second, says :—" It was also a day of very astonishing apparitions, both in the firmament and upon the earth, which I can instruct the truth of. As first, before the gospel was sent to the fields and desert places, in the year 1668, or 1669, in these places where the gospel was most frequently preached afterwards, how surprising and astonishing was the sight, both by night and day, of brae-sides covered with the appearance of men and women, with tents, and voices heard in them? Particularly, the first night that Mr John Dickson preached in the fields in the night-time, east from Glasgow, upon Clide's side, his parish being on the south side, Ruthglen, where he was settled minister before the unhappy restoration; and, after long persecution and imprisonment in the Bass and other places, was resettled there again, and died there since the Revolution. That first night, several people together, before they came to the appointed place, they saw upon their way a brae-side covered with the appearance of people, with a tent, and a voice crying aloud, 'This is the everlasting gospel; if ye follow on to know, believe, and embrace this gospel, it shall never be taken from you;' when they came to join them, all disappeared. Other companies of people in another way going there, heard a charming sweet sound of singing the 93d psalm, which obliged them to stand still until it was ended; other people who stayed at home, in several places, some heard the singing of the 44th psalm, others the 46th psalm. When the people who were there came home, they who stayed at home said, 'Where have ye been so long? for the preaching was near-by, for we heard the psalms sweetly sung, and can tell you a note of the sermon, which was the foresaid note.' Worthy Mr John Blackadder, who was a blest instrument, to the experience of many after this, who used to call these years the *blink*, was at all pains to examine the most solid Christians in that bounds, upon their hearing and seeing these things, who all asserted the truth of the same; and there are some yet alive, worthy of all credit, who heard the said Mr Blackadder, after this, discoursing with the foresaid Mr Dickson in Borrowstounness, in the house of Skipper William Horn, that old exercised, singular, self-denied, tender Christian, which is very rare to be found now. Mr Dickson was modest, being preacher himself that night; but Mr Blackadder concluded that it was of the Lord, and that the gospel would go to the fields, and be blest with power and success there. A daughter of the said Mr Blackadder, worthy of all credit, yet alive at Edinburgh, declares she heard her father relate the same to her mother, with chearfulness.

"*2dly*, Before the gospel came to that known place, Craigmad, where it became frequent afterwards, to the sweet experience of some yet alive; it lies within the shire of Stirling, and betwixt the parish of Falkirk and Moranside. How many did see that know, or brae-side, as close covered with the appearance of men and women? as they many times saw it afterwards; particularly, one day Alexander Stirling, who lived in the Redden, near that place, a solid, serious, zealous Christian, who told this several times to some yet alive, worthy of all credit, who told me of it, 'That he, with some others, one day was in that desert place, and saw that brae-side closs covered with the appearance of men and women, singing the 121st psalm, with a milk-white horse, and blood-red saddle on his back, standing beside the people,' which made that serious, discerning, observing Christian conclude, that the gospel would be sent to that place, and that the white horse was the gospel, and the red saddle persecution.

"*3dly*, That known place, Darmead, where the gospel was more frequent afterward than any place I know betwixt Clidesdale and Lothian, for which it was called the Kirk of Darmead, five parishes met about it, the like was seen there singing the 59th psalm. And whoever will consider these foresaid psalms, will see how suitable they were to these dispensations, and were oft sung by the Lord's suffering people in that time; but this brutish carnal age knows not what it is to syllable the Scriptures, or feed upon them."

At this period, too, the royalists were believed by the adverse party to be as much devoted to Satan as to King Charles the Second. The bishops were cloven-footed, and had no shadows;

the military officers who were employed to pursue the whigs into their lurkingplaces, wore coats of proof, and bestrode horses that could clamber among rocks like foxes; and the justices of peace commissioned to try the fugitives, were seen familiarly conversing with the foul fiend, to whom one in Dumfries-shire actually offered up his first-born child immediately after birth, stepping out with it in his arms to the staircase, where the devil stood ready, as it was suspected, to receive this innocent victim.

The curates also were, many of them, little better than wizards, if we may trust to Kirkton, and other authors of his persuasion, while the Episcopalians now and then retorted the accusation upon their adversaries. During this prevalence of magic, the Duke of Rothes was said to have been bewitched by Lady Anne Gordon, who accompanied him during his progresses in male attire, though one is tempted to think, if the lady could forget her dignity so far, that the enchantment was on the duke's side. (See Appendix, Note 9.) Dreams, too, were prevalent, revealing to tories the haunts of the hillmen, and to these the approach of their triumphant enemies. In God's Judgements against Persecutors, is recorded the dismal end to which so many of these reprobates came, among whom General Dalyell is said to have expired with a glass of wine at his lips, drinking the king's health, no doubt; Sir Robert Lawrie to have fallen from his horse, and had his neck broken, though that misfortune, in truth, belonged to his son; Sir George Mackenzie's body was wasted by fountains of blood continually issuing from all parts; nay, soon after death, the devil carried away Sir Archibald Kennedy of Colzean's remains in a fearful tempest; and the Duke of Queensberry's soul was seen, in a black coach drawn by six black horses, driving into Mount Vesuvius, a loud voice shouting out,—" Open to the Duke of Drumlangrig!" which proves, by the way, that the devil's porter is no herald. In fact, the legend is borrowed from the story of Antonio the Rich, in George Sandys's Travels. Jacob Bee, a citizen of Durham, notes in his MS. Diary—"John Borrow departed this life the 17th day of January, being Satterday, this yeare 1684-5, and was reported yt he see a coach drawn by 6 swine, all black, and a black man satt upon the cotch-box; he fell sick upon't, and dy'd, and of his death severall apparitions appeared after."

A ghost, whose history even to this hour inspires terror at many a cottager's fireside in Dumfries-shire, may perhaps, with propriety, be arranged among the spectral molestations which appalled the Scottish lieges in King Charles the Second's reign.—Sir Alexander Jardine of Applegirth had confined in the dungeon of his tower of Spedlins, a fellow named Porteous, by trade a miller, suspected of having wilfully set fire to his own premisses—suddenly called away to Edinburgh, the key of the vault travelled with the forgetful baron and Porteous died of hunger before the oversight was discovered. It is said that famine constrained him to devour one of his own hands; and some steps of a stair within the small dungeon are still shown, on which he was found stretched out in this deplorable condition; but it is surprising enough, that a pretty large window still remains, through which food might easily have been conveyed to the starving miller. Be that as it may, no sooner was the man dead than his ghost began to torment the whole household, so that no rest was to be had within the Tower of Spedlins either by day or night. In this dilemma, Sir Alexander, according to old use and wont, summoned a whole army of ministers to his aid, and by their strenuous efforts, Porteous was at length confined to the scene of his mortal agonies, where, however, he continued to scream of a night,—" Let me out, let me out; I'm dying of hunger!"—to flutter like a bird against the door of the vault, and to remove the bark from any twig that was sportively thrust through the keyhole. In the Appendix to the first volume of the Border Minstrelsy, is a very humorous poem, printed from the Bannatyne MS., called, "Ane Interlude of the Laying of a Gaist." The spell which thus compelled the spirit to remain in bondage, was attached to a large black-letter Bible, used by the exorcists, and afterwards deposited in a stone niche, which still remains in the wall of the stair-case; and it is certain that after the lapse of many years, when the family repaired to a newer mansion, built on the opposite side of the river Annan, the Bible was left behind to keep the restless spirit in order. On one occasion, indeed, the volume requiring to be re-bound, was sent half-way into Edinburgh, but the ghost, getting out of the dungeon, and crossing the river, made such a disturbance in the new house, hauling the baronet and his lady out of their bed, that the Bible was immediately recalled, and placed in its former situation. Of late times, it is no longer to be seen, and of the ghost no recent tidings have been heard. But a circumstance respecting one of the personages connected with this story, may here be recorded, as a great wonder in its own way, and at that superstitious period, deemed more marvellous than even the apparition of Porteous itself.—Lady Margaret Douglas, sister of William first Duke of Queensberry, and wife of Sir Alexander Jardine, was so extremely penurious in her temper, that she generally went abroad covered with rags; and so anxious was this lady to amass money, that she would sit for whole days on the bank of the river Annan, which flows near Spedlins, to carry people across upon her shoulders, for the moderate remuneration of a halfpenny. It may be justly enough suspected, that she had the sustenance of Porteous committed to her management during Sir Alexander's absence in Edinburgh.

In the year 1683, a young girl, in the parish of Monzie, Perthshire, after having suffered greatly from witchcraft, had some wonderful revelations, carefully recorded in a MS. preserved by Wodrow. From this several extracts are subjoined, much blasphemous folly being of course omitted.

"A Relation of a rare Providence that befell a young Childe, daughter to a Husband Man, or Farmorer, whose name is Donald M'Grigor, dwelling in the Parochin of Monzie, living within the Sheriffdome of Perth :—The child being about the age of ten years, and was bewitched by some woman upon the account of envy conceived against her father beforenamed, who, by his earnest and assiduous prayers, and the prayers of some of his acquaintance whom he invited to join with him in supplicating God to deliver his child from the power of Satan and his instruments, there was a wonderful deliverance granted; the history whereof has been attested by many credible witnesses, and especially her wonderfull speeches in the trances, is attested by a religious gentleman, and a considerable heritor in that paroch, named James Campbell of Monzie, who, pairtlie by himself, and pairtlie from his honest neighbours and acquaintance whom he trusts, received the relation and history of that mercifull dispensation of Providence; and from him the writter heirof received his notes heirof in write, which he thinks himself bound in conscience to publish, so far as in him lyes.

"Upon the 24th of September, 1683, the child, a daughter to Donald M'Grigor, was coming to her father's house from ane other house, a little distant from her father's house, about 8 hours at night, following her brother a little way behind him, and waxing fearfull, she began to run to overtake him, and then heard something cry not far of like ane owle; for haste she fell, and being more affraid, continued so till the 4th of January, 1684, and then began to see a man coming into her with a woman in every hand; the man was covered with a shirt to the ground; the women she could not know at the first. The man offered her a dollar if she would go with him, which she refused constantly; this they did 3 or 4 nights. Then the women said, 'We will take ane other course if she will not take it;' then about the 6th of January the two women appeared alone, with a bone of a horse head, whereof they made a picture, covering it with clay; then immediately appeared a black man, and sometimes he appeared like an ox. They desired him to make them a naile to put in the head of the picture, and he should have the child for whom the picture was made, which he did, the childe being all this time exceedingly affrighted, and calling to those y^t were in the house to take them from her, but they saw nor heard nothing; then the child thought she saw them put the picture betwix two fires for some space, during which time she was sore tormented; then they removed a little, and she had some ease; then they putt it in the fire again, and the child was in a sore torment, and exceeding hott and affrighted. Thus she was five or six times that night, and thus she was from that night, being the 8th of January, untill the 10th of February, taking some nights 8 fitts, some nights 10 or 12, and was ordinarly from 7 or 8, to 10 or 12 at night, seeing them, and tormented by fitts, as said is; and she heard the women say, 'That they rather had the father than the child.'" Many more circumstances are here omitted to be recorded.

"The way of the child her recovery.—Her father, Donald M'Grigor, being exceedingly grieved with so hard a providence, and dayly praying to God earnestly for his daughter's recovery all this time, and seeking the help of some by physick, it was told him that such means would do her no good, but a number of godly persons to pray for her was more suitable: so he, being earnest thereuntill, invited severall praying persons, to whom he communicate his trouble, about the 6th of February, to deal earnestly with God, which they did; and at the 10th of February, at night, they waiting on her according to the former manner, at the 6th fit of torment she apprehended that she did see a white hand, so exceedingly white, that she never did see any thing before so white, coming in betwixt her and them, whereupon she did see the devill starting backward as affraid; whereupon she heard a voice saying,—'Be not affraid for them; for if you learn the word of God, you shall be no more troubled with them, for you belong not to them, but to me.' The devill replyed, 'That he cared not, he had many better.' Then the hand did take the picture from the old woman, and dashed it to a stone. Then the old woman said to the devill, 'Wel, wel, this is not the way I expected this should be; I see we must leave off this;' whereupon the devill, the old woman, and her daughter, joyned hands as if they had been going to dance, and so parted and vanished. Whereupon the childe said, 'God be thanked, I think I shall never be troubled with yonder folk any more;' and her mother hearing her say so, said, 'I wish it be so; but how know you that?' To this the child answered, 'A voice hath told me;' whereupon the child did sing the two first verses of the 23d psalm, and it is to be remembered, she could not say a word of it before that time; nor in her former trouble could she be made to say, God help me, all the time they tormented her, altho several times she was commanded by the Laird of Monzie, and her parents and others, but could never obey."

She then, in her trances, began to converse with angels; they came to her nightly, and talked a great deal of stuff. "Thir angells had sometimes white feathers in their hands like wings. She told her father that they commanded her to learn the 11th psalm, &c. She asked, 'May they (the devils I suppose) not easily get advantage of my father, he goes not to the kirk —(note that he was a nonconformist)—O, what folk are these that go not to kirk?' To this they answered, 'They may be much better than these who go to kirk; and ye ought not to call them whiggs, but of the true catholick church.' Upon a time, her mother desired her daughter to spear at these angells who appeared to her, what came of young children not baptized, for her mother thought they could not go to heaven. They answered, 'That some of them may go to hell as wel as others.' The child also told, that in the time of her trouble she did see the devill, having a pig betwixt his feet and oyl in it, wherewith she did see him putt some thereof with his hand on the forehead of the two women."

After this the angels carried her in spirit to heaven, where (*horresco referens*) she was seated beside our blessed Saviour, whose conversations with her are recorded at much length. "Several of her neighbours said to her that she was taken away with the fairies, and that it was but the devil yet that was dealing with her." In heaven she saw Adam, "exceeding glorious, with a crown upon his head;" and by and by "Job, whom she said was most beautifull of all, and many others." She was told, "that when she was tormented, that she thought she saw the old woman and her daughter, and the black man, in her father's house; but they were in their own house; and whereas she thought they put the picture 'twixt two fires, it was 'twixt two coals only, and that the old woman had ane inchanted stick fastened to the picture, wherewith she put the picture in the fire when the child took her fitts, and took it out of the fire when she had ease; and when they went to their work, the old woman sate next the wall of the house, having the picture; the devil sat next, and then the daughter; and that all the house knew of it except two; and that the old man made a thing like a man's finger within her father's house, thereby to destroy the child and a part of all that he had, but was not suffered to put it there; and that she had put the devil under her father's threshold, that the devil might have the first that went over it, which was the old woman's son."

"She was desired to speir, 'Whether the indulged ministers did well in accepting the indulgence, or those that refused to hear them did worse in so doing, or those they called Cameronians, in that they did?' To all which she received no answer, though she often repeated the question. At length, she said, 'It is a strange thing none can make you tell any thing but what you please.' Then she was desired to speir, if it was allowable in us to take the Test, for all the great men had taken it; and if they would not do it, they would hang or banish them? After she asked this, answered, 'Take it not at all.' She said, 'Some great folk have taken it.' To this answered, 'The poor will go to heaven as soon as they.' She said, 'They will take their heads that refuse it?' To this answered, 'That matters not, tho' it were the night before the morn, if they go to heaven.' 'They may soon have their heads taken off, and go to heaven that speak against the Test?' Answered, 'They are not bound to do that neither.' Some space before that time there was a conformist minister execute for murder, which he denied to the last that he had any accession to it. She was desired to ask, 'If he had any hand in the childe's blood who was murdered?' It was answered, 'That he was guilty of that murder.' Then said she, 'How can that be, for I saw him pray and sing a psalm at his death?' To this it was answered, 'Notwithstanding, that doth not make any innocent of those things which they have done.' Then she said, 'That she heard him deny it.' To this answered, 'It was no good that bad him do that.'" This alludes to Duncan, the curate of Kinfauns, executed for the supposed murder of a child produced by his own maid-servant.—See Kirkton's *History*, p. 187. After some time, the girl took no more trances, and her angels left her. It does not appear what became of her subsequently.

Long before this affair there must have been a very celebrated witch in that neighbourhood, as Montgomery, giving an account of Polwarth's infancy, and his discovery by the weird sisters, says—

"Syne backward on horseback bravely they bendit,
That cam-nosed cocatrice they quite with them carry,

To Kait of Crief in a creil soon they gar send it,
Where seven year it sat baith singid and sairie."

There is a tradition current in Perthshire, that a witch who had been nurse to one of the antient and honourable family of Inchbrakie, was strangled and burnt on a hill called the Knock of Crieff, near her own cave, a small hole in the rock, still to be seen. This woman, whose names were Catharine Niven, (the last probably bestowed by her neighbours from that of the Fairy Queen) when led forth to the stake, is said to have spit from her mouth a small blue stone, which she gave to her foster-child, the Laird of Inchbrakie, telling him, that while the stone was preserved by him and his heirs, the house should flourish. This jewel was set in a ring, and is still in the possession of the family.

"In the year 1683," says Patrick Walker, "there was such a long and great frost, that from November to the middle of March, there was no labouring of the ground; yet even before the snow fell, when the earth was as iron, how many graves were in the west of Scotland, in desert places, in ones, twos, threes, fours, fives together, which was no imaginary thing; many yet alive who measured them with their staves, exactly the deepness, breadth, and length of other graves and the lump of earth lying whole together at their sides, which they set their feet upon, and handled them with their hands, which many concluded afterwards did presage the two bloody slaughter years that followed, 1684, 1685, when 82 of the Lord's suffering people were suddenly and cruelly murdered in desert places, wherever that heaven-daring enemy found them, and few to make graves or bury them, for fear of that enemy, who left their dead corps where they killed them."

CHAPTER VIII.
(A.D. 1684 TO A.D. 1718.)

Witchcraft in Dumfriesshire—Jonet Fraser's Remarkable Revelations—Additional Incidents in 1687—The Rev. T. Forrester's Dream—Showers of Hats, Guns, and Swords near Lanark—The Viscount Dundee's Ghost—The Renfrewshire Witches—The Pittenweem Witches—Spirits Troubling the House of the Minister of Kinross.

IN the year 1684, a Dumfries-shire woman, of the Presbyterian church, pretended to some wonderful visions, still extant in a MS., entitled,—"*Admiranda et Notanda.* Ane Account of strange and remarkable Revelations which were revealed to a Christian Friend in the Shire of Drumfrice, in the place aftermentioned, both anent the particular Ecstacies of her Spirit, but more anent the Case of the Church severall wayes. Before we shall begin to write of the same, we shall sett down some things of the person's extasie, both as to the manner and continuance of her extasies:—

"The person is a young woman, unmarried, of the age of about twenty years, whose name is Jonet Fraser, or, as we in the south use to pronounce it, Frissel, who then lived, and yet lives, with her father, Thomas Frissell, a weaver to his trade, a man of unblamed conversation in the sheriffdome of Drumfrice, in the countrey thereof called Nithisdale, and parochin of Closeburn, six miles, or thereby, from the town of Drumfriece.

"She is, and hath been for a long time, a person, in the judgment of all that know her, a serious Christian; and was for a good time before this befell her, more then ordinary exercised in private condition with God, as the relation afterspecified gives the reader a little touch.

"She can read print, but cannot write herself; but whatever she saw in vision, was att times able to give ane exact account of it, after all was over; and accordingly did give the relation following to some creditable gentlemen, and some country people, her acquaintance:—

"The time of my exercise was eight years, and all this time was troubled with the appearance of a thing like a *bee*, and other times like a black man, and that also at severall times, and in severall places.

"Then at the end of the eight year, I being at prayer, the black man did appear as at other times, he being upon the one side of me, and there appearing upon the other side a bonny hand and a rod in it, and the rod was budding; and I said, 'Is that thy hand and thy rod, O Lord?' And I was content to embrace the one, and flee the other. Then, upon that night eight nights, I coming home near hand unto my dwelling, I grew very drowsie, and fella sleep, and there was a voice said to me, 'Awake, why sleepest thou?' And there was lightning round about me; and I looking up to the top of a bush that was at my hand, there was the shape of a dove that went alongst with me in company to the house.

"Then, about three quarters of a year thereafter, the rod appeared again to be a double rod, or a rod that was springing and forthcoming; and after that time I was never troubled with the black man any more."

Her first revelation was on the 4th of June, 1684, but it is very difficult to make out what her visions portended. "On the 5th day of November, 1684, I being at prayer, there appeared unto me, in a bodily shape, three persons, (as to my sight all in white) and they goe round about me the way the sun goeth; their coming was still after one manner, when I was at my duty, only I discerned he that spoke first at one time, spoke first at all times, and so continued to speak by course, with Scripture notes, naming books, chapter, and verse, sometimes all the verse, sometimes a part." She was greatly concerned about the *suffering remnant*, and had many mysterious responses as to that. This intercourse with spirits continued for some years, and is very circumstantially detailed in the MS. At the conclusion of which is this additional miracle:—

"Besides what the reader has had formerly, he has likewise this following account of a passage that befell this holy woman, the 1st May, 1687, which was Sunday. This Jonet Frazer, and a young lass, a sister daughter of hers, about 17 or 18 years of age, having gone out into the fields, and both of them lying down on the grass near the water of Nith, which is but a bow-draught from her father's house, and both of them reading upon their Bibles, and lying about the distance of four yards the one from the other, this Jonet Frazer is taken with a great drouth, and goes to the water of Nith to take a drink, leaving her Bible open at the place where she was reading, which was the 34th chap. of Esaiah, from verse 5 to 11, inclusive, which begins,—' For my swoord, shall be bathed in heaven, behold it shall come down on the people of Idumea, and upon the people of my curse, to judgement,' &c. And when she had returned immediately as shoon as she could take a drink of water, she sees her Bible is coloured with bloud, as she thought, though afterwards, upon inspection and tryall, it was not bloud, but red as bloud, and such as no person by the colour could discern from bloud; upon which she asks the other lass, 'If any thing had been near her Bible?' And she answered, 'Nothing that she saw.' She asks, 'How could it then be that her Bible was covered over with bloud?' Which both of them going near, found to be the very same place where Jonet was reading, viz. from verse 5 to 11, and some farther of the 34th chap., so as the print was not at all legible. The other lass would have her wipe off the bloud, but she could not, but carried it as it was to her father, and a brother of hers, a godly young man, who is dead since, and some others, and did show it to them, who were curious to taste it, and it had a welsh taste, as if it had been some metear; the hens and birds would not pick it up.

"The very next Lord's day, 8th May, this Jonet beingin her father's barn about ane hour, alone, some little time before sunset, she came to the door of the barn to read, and while she was reading, about the 49th verse of Jeremiah, the like bloud did cover all that place which she was reading, viz. from the 46th verse to the 54th, as I remember, so thick as it marred all the print, and made it unintelligible, nor did she ever perceive it fall down upon the book, or observe it till it did cover and spread over all that place; and it is to be remarked, she was standing within the door, the thatch of the barn being over her head and over the book that she was reading on, and that the bloud covered the print in the very time wherein she was reading, it spread over that part of it.

"The very next Sabbath thereafter, 15th of May, while she is again in that same barn, reading the 14th chapter of Revelations, the like bloud fell on the book, and covered all the chapter from the 9th verse to the end of the chapter, in the very act of the reading it, and which, she said, that she perceived it not, but about half ane inches distance from the book before it fell down upon it.

"The relater heirof is Maister Henry Maxwell, of Dalswinton, who dwells within two miles of the place where she dwells; saw the Bible, and the bloud upon all the three places of that Bible, which is still extant.

"It is not bloud, for it is as tough as glew, and will not be scrapt off by a knife as bloud will;

but it is so like bloud as none can discern any difference by the colour."

After this course of visions and bloody showers, Mrs. Frazer, it would appear, fell under the suspicion of dealing with evil in place of good spirits. For in the year 1691, she was called before the presbytery, and confessed, " That she pretended to prophecying and seeing of visions, and that she had sinned greatly in being deluded by Satan, causing her prophecie and see things future." Her book was appointed to be examined by two of the presbytery; and on her second appearance she acknowledged that she was possessed by some evil spirit, and humbly besought the prayers of the ministers, and of all others; upon which the further examination of herself and the witnesses was delayed, and we hear no more of her.

In " A brief Account of the Rev. Mr Thomas Forrester, Minister at Alva, &c." extant among the Wodrow MS., is the following anecdote respecting an extraordinary dream:—" In the year 1684, when the persecution was very hot, Mr F. was among others that were intercommuned, and went over to Holland, and the next year came over with the Earl of Argyle, in the same ship with him. He told me, that the first night he slept aboard, he dreamed that all the persons in the ship were fled, which made a great impression upon him, but he told it to none, for fear of discouraging them." What follows is transcribed, as showing how early Argyle and his friends disagreed with regard to the plan of their unfortunate attempt:—" He told me, that Polwart, Sir John Cochrane, and others, the chief persons concerned in that expedition, were displeased with the earl's conduct, but did not know how to signifie so much unto him, and therefore pitched upon Mr Forrester, at whose hand they expected he would best take it; accordingly, he told the earl with all the caution he could; and the answer he got from him was,—' *Ne sutor ultra crepidam.*' Mr Forrester, turning from him in a little pett, he took him by a button of his coat, and told him, ' That he did nothing in all their affairs but by advice from those who were to land at that time in England.' "

" In the year 1686," says Walker, " especially in the months of June and July, many yet alive can witness, that about the Crossfoord-boat, two miles beneath Lanark, especially at the Mains, on the water of Clyde, many people gathered together for several afternoons, where there were showers of bonnets, hats, guns, and swords, which covered the trees and ground; companies of men in arms marching in order upon the water-side; companies meeting companies going all through other, and then all falling to the ground and disappearing, and other companies appearing the same way. I went there three afternoons together, and, as I could observe, there were two of the people that were together saw, and a third that saw not; and though I could see nothing, yet there was such a fright and trembling upon these that did see, that was discernable to all from these that saw not. There was a gentleman standing next to me, who spake, as too many gentlemen and others speak, who said, '*A pack of damned witches and warlocks that have the second sight, the devil ha't do I see,*' and immediately there was a discernable change in his countenance, with as much fear and trembling as any woman saw there, who cried out,—'*O, all ye that do not see, say nothing, for I perswade you it is matter of fact, and discernable to all that is not stone blind;*' and these that did see, told what works the guns had, and their length and wideness, and what handles the swords had, whether small or three-barred, or Highland guards; and the closing knots of the bonnets, black or blue; and these did see them there, wherever they went abroad, saw a bonnet and a sword drop in the way. I have been at a loss ever since, what to make of this last."

Walker, in what he calls his Postcript to the Life of Peden, is very angry with the sceptical persons, who threw ridicule upon this passage.

"But that," says he, "which the learned criticks and head-strong wits of young ministers and expectants quarrel most, and have upbraided me to my face for, is that 7th apparition at the Crosfoord boat, in the month of June and July, in the year 1686, two miles beneath Lanark, which, I say, I was there 3 days together and saw nothing; which is all matter of fact, and the naked verity, which I am only ambitious of in all my relations. But will these wild-ass colts tell me what stopped the eyes of the long clear-sighted Balaam, that saw a star to rise out of Jacob, a clear prophecy of the coming of the Messias, and yet saw not the angel standing with a drawn sword in his hand, and his dull ass saw him and stopt three times? And what stopped the eyes of the men who were with Daniel at the river Hiddekel, when he saw the vision, but they saw not, but greatly quaked? And what stopped the ears of Paul's companions in wickedness, going the devil's errand to Damascus, that saw the light and made them fall to the ground, but heard not the words of the voice that spoke to him? And what stopt the ears and the eyes of the captain of the Castle of Edinburgh, who was alarmed three times at night while the centinels were with him, but when they were sent off, he both saw and heard the different beating of drums, both English and Scots, in that strange apparition in the year 1650, before the English came to it?"

After the battle of Killicranky, where fell the last hope of James in the Viscount of Dundee, the ghost of that hero is said to have appeared, about daybreak, to his confidential friend, Lord Balcarras, then confined to Edinburgh Castle on suspicion of jacobitism. The spectre, drawing aside the curtain of the bed, looked very stedfastly upon the earl; after which it moved towards the mantle-piece, remained there for some time in a leaning posture, and then walked out of the chamber without uttering one word. Lord Balcarras, in great surprise, though not suspecting that which he saw to be an apparition, called out repeatedly to his friend to stop, but received no answer; and subsequently learnt, that at the very moment this shadow stood beside him, Dundee had breathed his last near the field of Killicranky.

Lord Balcarras's first wife was Lady Mauritia de Nassau de Beverwaert, daughter of the Lord of Beverwaert, &c. a natural son of Maurice Prince of Orange. At her marriage, the bridegroom having forgot to prepare a ring, and borrowed one from a friend in the company, it proved a mourning ring, with a death's-head on it; this made such an impression upon the lady, that she declared she could not live, and her prediction was speedily fulfilled, as she died of her first child in less than a year after her marriage.—Lindsay's *Memoirs, MS.* To this anecdote may be added some uncommon circumstances still remembered respecting the death of Grace, Countess of Aboyne and Moray, who, in her early youth, had the weakness to consult a celebrated fortune-teller, inhabiting an obscure close of Edinburgh. The sibyl predicted, that she would become the wife of two earls, and how many children she was to bear; but withal assured her, that if she should see a new coach of a certain colour driven up to her door as belonging to herself, her hearse must speedily follow. Many years afterwards, Lord Moray, who was not aware of this prediction, resolved to surprise his wife with the present of a new equipage; but when Lady Moray beheld from a window a carriage of the ominous colour arrive at the door of Tarnaway, and heard that it was to be her own property, she sank down, exclaiming that she was a dead woman, and actually expired in a short time after. 17th Nov. 1738.

In the year 1697, occurred the trial and condemnation of many persons for bewitching Christian Shaw, a girl about eleven years of age, the daughter of John Shaw of Bargarran. The particulars of this comic tragedy were collected by John MacGilchrist, town-clerk of Glasgow, and embodied in a pamphlet written by Mr Francis Grant, advocate, afterwards a knight, and lord of session, with the style of Lord Cullen. The title of the work runs thus:—"A True Narrative of the Sufferings and Relief of a Young Girle, strangely molested by Evil Spirits, and their Instruments in the West; collected from authentick Testimonies thereanent," &c. To sum up a long story in a few words, the young girl, who seems to have been antient in wickedness, having had a quarrel with one of the maidservants, pretended to be bewitched by her, and forthwith began, according to the common practice in such cases, to vomit all manner of trash; to be blind and deaf on occasion; to fall into convulsions, and to talk a world of nonsense, which the hearers received as the quintessence of afflicted piety. By degrees, a great many persons were implicated in the guilt of the maid-servant, and no less than twenty were condemned, of whom five suffered death on the Gallo Green of Paisley; and one man, John Reid, strangled himself in prison, or, as the report went, was strangled by the devil, lest, says Crauford, in his History of Renfrewshire, "he should make a confession to the detriment of the service." Yet he seems to have confessed abundantly, for he gave a long account of his first interview with Satan, to whose meetings he and the haggs were summoned by a black dog with a chain about his neck, the tinkling of which they followed; and affirmed that the foul fiend gave them a morsel of an unchristened child's liver to eat, as a sovereign remedy against confession when apprehended; but John did not swallow his portion, which, without doubt, was the reason of his subsequent ingenuity. "I own," says the Rev. Mr Bell, in his MS. Treatise on Witchcraft, "there has been much harm done to worthy and innocent persons in the common way of finding out witches, and in the means made use of for promoting the discovery of such wretches, and bringing them to justice; that oftentimes old age, poverty, features, and ill fame, with such like grounds, not worthy to be represented to a magistrate, have yet moved many to suspect and defame their neighbours, to the unspeakable prejudice of Christian charity; a late instance whereof we had in the west, in the business of the sorceries exercised upon the Laird of Bargarran's daughter, anno 1697, a time when persons of more goodness and esteem than most of their calumniators were defamed for witches, and which was occasioned mostly by the forwardness and absurd credulity of diverse otherwise worthy ministers of the gospel, and some topping professors in and about the city of Glasgow."

These Renfrewshire witches were said to have

roasted the effigy of Mr Hardy, a clergyman, after having dipt it into a mixture of ale and water, a circumstance not general in that sort of cookery. Miss Shawe, the heroine of this romance, afterwards acquired a remarkable dexterity in spinning of yarn, which she manufactured into thread; and it was from her attempts, aided by a friend who had learnt some secrets as to the process when in Holland, that the extensive manufacture of thread in Renfrewshire originated. About the year 1718, she became the wife of Mr Miller, minister at Kilmaurs. It may be observed, that the delusion, of which this wretched girl was the cause, had a shocking prototype in the madness (for it can be esteemed nothing less) concerning sorcery, that possessed New England in the year 1690. The reader is referred to Mather's pamphlets for the details, among which the confessions are abundantly ridiculous. From one of these, but of a prior date, it would appear that *Brownie* had made his way to New England. Mary Johnson tried upon an indictment of familiarity with the devil, confessed " that a devil was wont to do her many services. Her master once blamed her for not carrying out the ashes, and a devil did clear the hearth for her afterwards. Her master, sending her into a field to drive out the hogs that used to break into it, a devil would *scoure* them out, and make her laugh to see how he *feaz'd* 'em about," &c. See "The Witty and Entertaining Exploits of George Buchanan, commonly called the King's Fool," for an account of a Scottish Brownie, servant to an Italian lord, which George baptised by surprise. This was in Italy, and the spirit " went off weeping and crying, O, let never a rogue put trust in his own countryman after me."

The case of the Pittenweem witches, in the year 1704, excited a considerable degree of interest, as it involved the clerical debates of two ministers, one Episcopal, the other Presbyterian, and was marked with the barbarous murder of a poor woman, named Janet Cornfoot, who fell a victim to the spite of the clergyman, the indolence of the magistrates, and the fury of a brutish rabble. Her accuser, a fellow who pretended to take fits till he found them no longer profitable, *delated* her, together with Beatrix Laing, and other women, for having afflicted him with this disorder. Immediately the witches were seized, and several drunkards, as guards, set over them in prison, who, by dint of pricking, and keeping them from any repose, extorted confessions, afterwards retracted,—Cornfoot declaring, that the minister himself beat her with his staff in order to make her speak out. At last she managed an escape from confinement; but being caught and brought back to Pittenweem, the mob assailed her, and nobody attempting her rescue, she was hauled down to the beach, pelted with rubbish, swung in a rope betwixt a ship and the shore, and a heavy door being thrown upon her, over which stones were heaped, she was finally pressed to death. This horrible transaction gave rise to several pamphlets, criminating and defending the minister and the magistrates; but the murderers were never brought to justice. "Beattie Laing," says the continuator of Satan's Invisible World, " died *undesired* in her bed, in St. Andrews; and all the other witches died miserable and violent deaths."

With regard to mobbing, in the year 1628, Dr Lamb, a wizard who had been under the protection of the Duke of Buckingham, was torn to pieces by the London mob.—Wilson's *History*, p. 287. And, incredible to relate, on the 22d of April, 1751, a rabble of about 5000 persons beset the work-house at Tring, in Hertfordshire, where seizing Luke Osborne and his wife, two persons suspected of witchcraft, they ducked them in a pond till the old woman died. After which, her corpse was put to bed to her husband by the mob, of whom only one person was hanged for this detestable outrage.

In the year 1705, we learn from the Parochial Register of Spott, that many witches were burnt on the top of Spott Loan. In the same Record is this passage :—" 1698, the session, after a long examination of witnesses, refer the case of Marion Lillie, for imprecations and supposed witchcraft, to the presbytery, who refer her for trial to the civil magistrate. Said Marion generally called the *Rigwoody Witch*."

After which, the most remarkable event of the kind to be met with, is the supernatural molestation of a clergyman's house at Kinross, in the year 1718. This is recorded in a curious printed sheet, here subjoined entire, having for its title, " Endorism, or a strange Relation of Dreamers or Spirits that trouble the Minister's House of Kinross."

" Many deny that there are any such as witches, though we have it expressly contained in the Word of God, that there was a witch at Endor that Saul, in his distress, resorted to and communed with, but call them dreamers; these, I say, argument not so learnedly as politically, or for fear they or their relations should be sentenced for such ; as for instance, Bettie Laing, who was reckoned and confessed herself a witch, in the town of Pittenweem, before a whole congregation of people on the Sabbath-day, was brought off as a dreamer; for, said she, if they burn me, both ladies in coaches and sidans, who are equally guilty, must burn also; and accordingly, she and many others of her accomplices were set at liberty.

"However, tho' people should deny both spirit and angel, to be sure there are both spirits and angels good and bad; and according to Scripture, there may be witches, seeing there was a witch at Endor, let people say as they list; but what is the essence of spirits, or what way the devil makes use of these deluded creatures, or changes them into various shapes on occasion, is hard to determine. But without further prefacing, to declare unto the world how the house and family of Mr M'Gill, minister in Kinross, hath been for a considerable time troubled by spirits, or such beings as the more politick and refined sort of high-flyers call dreamers, it is hoped will neither be offensive to this minister or any of his relations, or disparagement, seeing the godly are the only objects of the devil's fury; for such as the devil is sure of, he does not heed them until he has them at once.

"The first occasion, then, of this gentleman's house and family being troubled was, that there was some silver spoons then and knives amissing, (as is reported) which were found in the barn among the straw sometime afterwards, stuck up in the floor, with a big dish, all nipped to pieces; after which time they could eat no meat but what was full of pins; as one day as the minister was eating of an egg, he found a pin in the egg, and mostly what meat they eat, they had still abundance of pins: wherefore the minister's wife would make ready a piece of meat herself, that she might be sure there was no deceit in the matter; but when it was presented to the table, there were several pins in it, particularly a big pin the minister used for his gown. Another day there was a pair of sheets put to the green among other peoples, which were all nipped to pieces, and none of the linnings belonging to others troubled. A certain night severals went to watch the house, and as one was praying, down falls the press, wherein was abundance of lime-vessels, all broke to pieces; also at one other time, the dreamers, or spirits as they call them, not only tore and destroyed the clothes that were locked up in a coffer to pieces, but the very laps of a gentlewoman's hood, as she was walking along the floor, were clipt away; as also a woman's gown-tail, and many other things not proper to mention. Moreover, a certain girl eating some meat, turned so very sick, that being necessitate to vomit, cast up five pins; also a stone thrown down the chimney, wambled a space in the floor, and then took a flight out at the window. Also there was thrown in the fire the minister's Bible, which would not burn; but a plate and two silver spoons thrown in, melted immediately; also what bread is fired, were the meal never so fine its all made useless, and many other things, which are both needless and sinful to mention. Now, is it not very sad that such a good and godly family should be so molested, that employ their time no other way but by praying, reading, and serious meditation, while others, who are wicked livers all their lifetime, and avowedly serve that wicked one, are never troubled.

"It's true, these bad spirits or dreamers have no power of their bodies, but they exceedingly disquiet the family; which, that the event may redound to God's glory, and this honest families good, ought to be the serious prayer of all good people. Printed, June 1718."

CHAPTER IX.

(A.D. 1718 to A.D. 1719.)

Curious Account of a case of Witchcraft in Caithness—James Fraser's letter to Wodrow—The Lord-Advocate's letter to the Sheriff-Depute, Caithness—The Sheriff's answer—William Montgomerie's Petition—Margaret Nin-Gilbert's Examination and Confession.

AMONG the Wodrow MSS. are some letters and other papers concerning a case of witchcraft which occurred in Caithness in the year 1718, As these have never been printed, and are extremely curious, they are subjoined.

To the Rev. Mr Robert Wodrow, Minister of the Gospel at Eastwood, near Glasgow.

Very Reverend dear Brother,

I longed much for an opportunity of sending you some informations that I promised you about witches and witchcraft. The most remarkable that has been of that kind in this country, is what happened in the parish of Redcastle, or Kilernan, where the poor man who was Episcopal minister in that place, lost his life by means of witchcraft. I caused a friend of mine to ask the gentleman who was sheriff-depute of Ross at that time, and who lives now near Inverness, where the best account of this matter might be had; but he said that the process, with all the papers and informations relating to it, was taken out of their hands by the king's advocate; and I reckon it's not impossible for yourself to procure these papers. The thing happened sometime I think in King William's reign. I shall endeavour, if you desire it, to send the exactest information that can be had from gentlemen and country people who remember it.

In the mean time, I send you inclosed information relating to a story of that nature that hapned much more lately in Caithness; I procured them by means of Alexander Frazer, at Scrabster, collector of the rents of that bishoprick, who is my uncle. There is the confession of Margaret Nin-Gilbert, or Gilbertson, attested, as I desired it should be, by the Rev. Mr Innes. There is a copy of Montgomerie's petition, a copy of the king's advocate, Mr. Dundas's letter to the shiref-depute, and his return.

My uncle, the above-mentioned gentleman, informs me farther, as follows: That Margaret Olson, mentioned in the information, was a tennant of his, whom he had removed for the wickedness of her behaviour, and put this William Montgomerie in her place. She was heard to threaten and curse him (Montgomerie); and a little time after her removal the house was infested in manner as the petition bears; that he was informed that Nin-Gilbert confessed privately that this Olson solicited her to do mischief to Mr Frazer, which she said she had no power nor inclination to do; but that one night as he was crossing a bridge, there was an attempt upon him, about which they were divided among themselves. He says he remembers perfectly well that his horse gave him a great deal adoe at that place, but that by the Lord's goodness he escaped. He says, which likewise I remember, that he had great sickness for five or six weeks about the time these people were catched, which, though it was the common story at that time, he will not hear imputed to them. He adds, that he thought this matter was the more carelessly managed that this Nin-Gilbert had been midwife to a certain great lady, and that the rest against whom she informed being put in the same prison with her, she was in a manner murdered; this you'll keep to yourself. Since I saw you in Edinburgh in May last, there has been great noise of witchcraft in the parish of Loth, in Sutherland, by which the minister is said to have suffered. He is not yet recovered; however, the thing has been examined into, and the women were, I know, before the presbytery. There was likewise very lately a rumour of that kind in the parish of Tarbat. If there is any thing in these stories, and that you desire to know more about them, I shall endeavour to procure the best information.

I presume to suggest this much with respect to the publication of these things, that mankind will not have such value for this subject as will make them be at great expence of time or money for it; but I reckon an exact, judicious, and compendious performance will be very acceptable to the world; nor know I any hand it is so likely to thrive in as yours. I shall be ambitious to serve you in this, and any thing else you shall command me, being, V. R. D. B. your affection brother and humble servant in the Lord,

JAMES FRASER.

Alness, in Ross, Aprile 18, 1727.

*The King's Advocate to the Sheriff-Depute of
  Caithness. Edinr. 5th March,* 1719.

Sir,

There are severall accounts come up here of very extraordinary, if not fabulous, discoveries of witchcrafts and using of poisons in your county, and severall of the persons are said to be in custody, I suppose by your warrand; if there be any truth in these stories, I might be surprised that you have transmitted no account of it to me. It is the part of every sherrif, when things of that kind fall out, I mean discoveries of high crimes, to transmit ane account of it to those whom his majesty is pleased to employ to look after these matters, it being our duty to advise both as to the proper method and court before which these things are to be prosecute, and to take care that crimes neither be shifted nor too rashly prosecute. I therefore give you the trouble of this to desire you, with the first opportunity, to transmitt to me full copies of the examination and declarations either of those persons who have been apprehended, or as partners in those malefices, or as evidence with relation to every particular fact which the declarations of the persons apprehended may have led you to enquire into; for I presume you know your duty so well as not to have neglected to take full examinations of every person who you could suspect was capable of giving you any light in the matter. I hope I need not put you in mind that you ought not to allow any person that may be mentioned by those wretches as accomplices, access to them, except in order to confront them, in presence of yourself and other persons of reputation. You will, I do not doubt, take care that none who are committed either be dismissed or suffered to make their escape till the matter be fully enquired into. There is some surmise here that you design to make a kind of tryall of it before your own court. I indeed give no credit to that, because I hope you know that a thing of that kind is both of too great difficulty to be tryed without very deliberate advice, and is above the jurisdiction of ane inferior court; and although you may think yourself in some speciall case, because of my Lord Broadalbine's pretence to a right of justiciary, yet you must know, at the same time, that that right never hath been acknowledged by the government, and I have ground to believe never will be. I have writt to the Earl of Caithness, desiring him, as justice of the peace, to concur with you in any examinations as he may think necessary, which I hope his lordship will comply with.

I am, Sir, your most humble servant,

Ro. Dundas.

Answer. Thurso, March 24th, 1719.

Honourable Sir,

I had your's, challenging me for not transmitting to you ane account of some witchcraft alledged committed lately in this country, which I acknowledge was my duty to have done; but exercising the office of sheriff only in the absence of the Earl of Broadalbine, and Ulbster, who are both at Edinburgh, I reckoned it presumption in me to transmit first the accounts to you, but directed them to be given to you. What information I can give is as follows:—In the month of December last, one William Montgomerie, mason, in Burnside of Scrabster, gave in a petition to the sheriff, representing that his house was severall times infested with cats to that degree, that he nor his family were in safety to reside there any longer, and particularly condescended, that upon the 28th of November last, and also five days thereafter, he had encountered with the saids cats in his house, and with his sword, and some other weapons, had killed two of them, and, as he apprehended, had wounded some more of them; and because ane woman in the neigbbourhood contracted sickness immediately after these encounters, craved ane warrand from the sherrif to inspect the woman, but could not condescend in his petition upon the person; and this representation seeming all the time to be very incredulous and fabulous, the sheriff had no manner of regard yrto. There was no farther thought of this affair from December, that the representation was not given in, intill the 12th of February last, that one Margaret Nin-Gilbert, in Owst, living about ane mile and ane half distant from Montgomery's house, was seen by some of her neighbours to drop at her own door one of her leggs from the midle, and she being under bad fame before for witchcraft, the legg, black and putrified, was brought to me; and immediately thereafter I ordered her to be apprehended and incarcerated; and she having been examined upon the 18th of February before me, and some ministers, and persons of reputation in the place, confessed her being in compact with the devil, and several others, as mentioned in her confession; and particularly, that the time condescended upon by Montgomerie in his petition, she was bodily present in his house, though she appeared to him in the likeness of a catt, and that her leg was broke by a stroke received from him; and condescended upon severall women who were present with her in Montgomerie's house that night, who were seized and continue imprisoned, except two, who dyed the night of the encounter with the catts in Montgomerie's house, or a few days thereafter. You have the copies of petitions and confessions inclosed. This Margaret Nin-Gilbert dyed in prison two weeks or thereby after emitting of her confession; and there are other three defamed by her who continues incarcerated, but notwithstanding of great pains taken upon them, cannot be brought to any confession, therefore have caused summond several persons to see what can be exhibited and made out against them; and after examination you may expect ane account of the Earle of Caithness, who will be acquainted of the dyet of examination of the saids persons, so that if his lordship will take the trouble, he may attain the same as justice of peace. There are, no doubt, information sent south of charms found with the said Margaret Nin-Gilbert, and that there were severall others defamed by her besides these seized; but as to the charms, I never saw nor heard of any found with her, nor was I present at her fyling of any person but those who are mentioned in her confession herewith sent you.

To the Sherrif-Deput of Caithness, the Petition of William Montgomery, Mason in the Burnside of Scrabster,

Humbly sheweth,

That your petitioner's house being infested with catts these three months bygone, viz. September, October, and November, to that degree that my wife was affrighted terribly att the fearfull and the unnaturall noise in my absence for most of these months forsaid at Mey, and sent five severall times for me to repair home, or else she would leave the house and flit to Thurso; and my servant-woman was so affrighted by the saids catts, that she left my service obreptly before term, and would by no means serve me longer; and your petitioner having returned home, was severall nights disturbed by these catts, and five of them one night at the fireside where the servant-woman only was, she cryed out, "The catts were speaking among themselves;" and particularly on Fryday the 28th of November, having got in at a hole in a chest, I then saw her, where I watched an opportunity to cut off her head when she put it out att the said hole, and having fastened my sword on her neck, which cutt her, nor could I hold her; (at last) having opened the chest, my servant, William Geddes, having fixed my durk in her hinder quarter, by which stroke she was fastened to the chest; yet after all she escaped out of the chest with the durk in her hinder quarter, which continued there till I thought, by many stroaks, I had killed her with my sword; and having cast her out dead, she could not be found next morning, though we arose early to see what had become of her. And farther, about four or five nights after,

my servant being in bed, cryed out, "That some
of these catts had come in on him;" and having
wrapt the plaid about the catt, I thrust my durk
through her belly, and having fixed the durk in
the ground, I drove all her head with the back
of ane axe untill she was dead, and being cast out,
could not be found next morning. Declares, that
both catts were dead in my apprehension, and
was throught with my durk, yet not one drop of
blood came from them. Further declares, That
after the strickest enquiry, none of these catts
belonged to any in the neigbourhood; the one
night I saw eight of them, and this looking like
witchcraft, it being threatened that none should
thrive in my said house, and being informed that
some person of bad fame fell sick immediately
upon the back of this, and continued to be affixed
to her bed, I earnestly desire the same person
may be inspected, in case any wounds be found on
her body. And your petitioner shall ever, &c.
Sic subr. (WILLM. MONTGOMERIE.) Decr. 1718.

*Thurso, 8th February, 1719 years. In presence
of Mr John Munro, Minister at Halikirk,
David Forbes, Bailzie of Thurso, Andrew
Balfour, Merchand there, James Maky, William Munro, and Andrew Munro, Merchands
there.*

The said day, Mr William Innes, minister of

Thurso, having interrogat Margaret Nin-Gilbert, who was apprehended Fryday last on suspicion of witchraft, as follows :—1*mo*, Being interrogat, If ever there was any compact between her and the devil ? Confessed, That as she was travelling some long time bygone, in ane evening, the devill mett with her in the way in the likeness of a man, and engaged her to take on with him, which she consented to ; and that she said she knew him to be the devil or he parted with her. 2*do*, Being interrogat, If ever the devil appeared afterwards to her ? Confessed, That sometimes he appeared in the likeness of a great black horse, and other times riding on a black horse, and that he appeared sometimes in the likeness of a black cloud, and sometimes like a black henn. 3*to*, Being interrogat, If she was in the house of William Montgomerie, mason in the Burnside of Scrabster, especially on that night, the —— day of ——, when that house was dreadfully infested with severall catts, to that degree that W. M. foresaid was obliged to use sword, durk, and ax in beating and fraying away these catts ? Confessed, That she was bodily present yr, and that the said M. had broke her legg either by the durk or ax, which legg since has fallen off from the other part of her body; and that she was in the likeness of a feltered catt, night forsaid, in the said house ; and that Margaret Olsone was there in the likeness of a catt also, who being stronger than she, did cast her on Montgomerie's durk when her leg was broken.

4*to*, Being interrogat, How she could be bodily present, and yet invisible? Declares, She might have been seene, but could give no account by what means her body was rendered invisible. She declares, That several other women were present there that night in the other end of the house. Being interrogat, How they came not to be seene, seeing they were not there in the likeness of catts, as were others condescended on? Declares, The devil did hide and conceall them by raising a dark mist or fog to skreen them from being seen. 5*to*, Being interrogat, Who more were present with her in that house the forsaid night? Confesses, That Margaret Olsone, spouse to Donald Barney, was present there bodily; *item*, and Jannet Pyper, spouse to David Mackryrie, was present there, with a red petticoat upon her; *item*, and that Helen Andrew, spouse to John Sinclair, in Owst, was present there, the said Helen Andrew being so wounded, and crushed and bruised, with either sword, ax, or durk, that she dyed the same night of her wounds, or few days yrafter; *item*, confessed that Margaret Callum, spouse to James More, now in Forss, was present there; and that —— M‘Huistan, spouse to William M‘Ky, in Skaill, was there present;

which —— M'Huistan, in a few days thereafter, was cast, or cast herself from the rocks of Borrowstoun into the sea, since which time she was never seen. As also being asked, If ever she was guilty of any malefice to any person? Denyed the same. 6to, Being interrogat, What brought her and her accomplices to Montgomerie's house? Answered, they were doing no harm there. To which Mr Innes replyed, that the disturbing and infesting a man's house with hideous noises, and cryes of catts, was a great wrong done to him, having a natural tendency to fright the family and children. The premisses are attested to be the ingenuous confession of Margaret Nin-Gilbert, *alias* Gilbertson, by William Innes, minister of Thurso.

Nota, That Margaret Callum foresaid, denying any former conversation with Nin-Gilbert, asked the said Nin-Gilbert, When she was in company with her? To which she replied, In her own house in Brims, when there were five or six hundred about the house, meaning devils and witches.

Nota, That upon a vulgar report of witches having the devil's marks in their bodies, Margaret Olsone being tryed in the shoulders, where there were severall small spots, some read, some blewish, after a needle was driven in with great force almost to the eye, she felt it not. Mr Inness,

Mr Oswald, ministers, and several honest women, and Bailzie Forbes, were witnesses to this. And further, that while the needle was in her shoulder, as foresaid, she said,—"Am not I ane honest woman now?"

CHAPTER X.

(A.D. 1720 TO A.D. 1724.)

Lord Torphichen's Son Bewitched—The Tinklerian Doctor—The last Execution of a Scottish Witch—The Statutes regarding Withcraft Repealed—The Elgin Wonder—The Minister of Salcraig—Rutherford's Revelations—The Laird of Cool's Ghost.

IN the year 1720, Patrick Sandilands, (third son of James Lord Torphichen) a mischievous boy, took it into his head to declare that some old women and a man in Calder had bewitched him; he fell down in trances, from which no horse-whipping could rouse him till he chose his own time to revive—pronounced prophesies—made urine the colour of ink—was lifted up into the air by invisible hands,—and, in fine, so worked upon the fears and affections of his family, that Lord Torphichen at length gave credit to the falsehoods he uttered, and his tormenters were seized. From circumstances, it is probable that the child's brain was disordered. The minister of the parish, and many others, quickly caught the infection;—a fast was proclaimed at Mid Calder, and the sermon preached on that occasion, by Mr John Wilkie, minister of the gospel at Uphall, was afterwards printed by desire of Lord Torphichen. At this discourse were present two of the confessing witches; and Wilkie, in his preface, says that three more subsequently acknowledged their guilt. To complete the assemblage of sages, William Mitchell, the mad Tinklerian Doctor, *alias* White Smith, sallied forth from his shop in the West Bow of Edinburgh, in order to exorcise the evil spirits at Calder. "I went," says he, "to Calder, the 14th day of January, 1720, before day-light, being eight miles, in ill weather, fasting, on my foot. I took the sword of the spirit at my breast, and a small wand in my hand, as David did when he went out to fight against Goliah; so I went to cast the devil out of my Lord Torphichan's son. So ye see that I was not lying in my letter that I wrote to Tillehewn, when I said Peter and I were two bold fellows. When I went to his house, his servants were eating and drinking, although he had appointed it to be a fast day, in order to get the devil out of his house. I do think they might have fasted untill the sermon was over upon such a weighty business; and they offered me some, but

I took neither meat nor drink of his. Some think it a fast day when they hear a minister preach for the payment.

"Then I went to my lord and said I was sent by God to come to cast out the devil out of his son, by faith in Christ. He seemed to be like that lord who had the charge of the gate of Samaria. Then I said to him, 'My lord, do ye not believe me?' Then he bad me 'go and speak to many ministers that was near by him;' but I said, 'I was not sent to them.' Then he went himself and spoke to them what I said, but they would not hear of it; so I went to three witches and a warlock to examine them in sundry places. Two of them denyed, and two of them confessed. I have no room here to relate all down that I said to them, and what they said; but I asked them, 'When they took on in that service?' The wife said, 'Many years;' and the man said, 'It was ten years to him.'

"Then I asked the wife, 'What was her reason for taking on with the devil?' And she said, 'He promised her riches, and she believed him.' Then she called him many a cheat and liar in my hearing. Then I went to the man, because he was a great professor, and could talk of religion with any of the parish, as they that was his neighbours said, and he was at Bothell-Bridge fighting against the king; and because of that I desired to ask questions at him, but my lord's officer said to me, his lord would not allow me; but I said I would not be hindered neither by my lord nor by the devil, before many there present. Then I asked, 'What iniquity he found in God that he left his service?' Then he got up, and said, 'O, sir, are ye the minister?' So ye see the devil knows me to be a minister better than the magistrates; and he said, 'He found no fault in God, but his wife beguiled him;' and he said, 'Wo be to the woman his wife,' and blamed her only as Adam did his wife, and the wife blamed the devil; so ye see it is so from the beginning. This is a caution to us all never to hearken to our wives except they have scripture on their side. Then I asked at him, 'Did he expect heaven?' 'Yes,' said he. Then I asked at him, 'If he could command the devil to come to speak to me?' But he said, 'No.' Then I said again, 'Call for him, that I may speak with him.' He said again, 'It was not in his power.' Then my lord sent more servants that hindered, me to ask any more questions, otherwise I might have seen the devil, and I would have spoken about his son."—Dr MITCHEL'S *strange and wonderful Discourse concerning the Witches and Warlocks in West Calder.*

In the Continuation of Satan's Invisible World are sundry particulars respecting these witches,

One of whom confessed that she gave her dead child to the devil to make a roast of. The boy whom they were supposed to have tormented, in more mature life became an excellent sailor; and having obtained the command of an East India vessel for his gallant conduct in repulsing a party of the pirate Angria's men, after they had boarded her, he finally perished in a storm.

The Tinklerian Doctor (referred to in the preceding), as he chose to be called, was a crazed white-iron smith, who imagined himself much wiser than the Archbishop of Canterbury, all the clergymen of his native country, and even the magistrates of Edinburgh! He printed a number of pamphlets and single sheets, full of very amusing nonsense, and generally adorned them with a wooden cut of the Mitchell Arms. In one of these, he gives a curious account of a journey which he made into France, where, he affirms, "the king's court is six times bigger than the king of Britain's; his guards have all feathers in their hats, and their horse tails are to their heels; and their king is one of the best-favoured boys that you can look upon,—blyth like, with black hair; and all his people, in general, are better natured than either the Scots or English, except the priests. Their women seem to be modest, for they have no farding-gales. The greatest wonder I saw in France was to see the bra' people sit down on their knees in the clarty ground, when the priest comes by carrying the cross, to give a sick person the sacrament. I have," continues this eminent divine and historian, "a good pennyworth of peuther spoons, fine like silver, none such made in Edinburgh; and silken pocks for wiggs, and French white pearl beads,—all to be sold for little or nothing." See "A part of the Works of the Eminent Divine and Historian, Doctor William Mitchell, Professor of Tinklarienism in the University of the Bow-Head, being a syse of Divinity, Humanity, History, Philosophy, Law, Physick; composed at various Occasions for his own satisfaction and the World's illumination," &c. One of his last productions was a pamphlet on the murder of Captain Porteous, which he concludes by saying,—"If the king and clergy gar hang me for writing this, I'm content, because it is long since any man was hanged for religion."

The last execution of a Scottish witch took place in Sutherland, A.D. 1722, the sentence having been pronounced by the sheriff-depute, Captain David Ross, of Little Dean. This old woman belonged to the parish of Loth, and among other crimes, was accused of having ridden upon her own daughter, transformed into a poney, and shod by the devil, which made the girl ever after lame, both in hands and feet, a misfortune entailed upon her son, who was alive of late years. The grandmother was executed at Dornoch; and it is said, that after being brought out to execution, the weather proving very severe, she sat composedly warming herself by the fire prepared to consume her, while the other instruments of death were making ready.

It is well known, that in the year 1735, the statutes against witchcraft, Scottish as well as English, were repealed; which gave so much offence to the *seceders* from the Established Church of Scotland, that in their annual Confession of National and Personal Sins, printed in an Act of their Associate Presbytery, at Edinburgh, 1743, are enumerated the Act of Queen Anne's Parliament for tolerating the Episcopal Religion in Scotland; the Act for Adjourning the Court of Session during the Christmas Holydays; *as also the Penal Statutes against Witches having been repealed by Parliament, contrary to the express Law of God!* With all the compassion, however, which the fate of so many unfortunate victims is calculated to excite, it ought not to be forgotten, that many of these persons made a boast of their supposed art, in order to intimidate, and extort from their neighbours whatever they desired; that they were frequently of an abandoned life, addicted to horrible oaths and imprecations; and in several cases venders of downright poison, by which they gratified their customers in their darkest purposes of avarice or revenge.

During this century, three pamphlets respecting heavenly revelations, and other wonders, were printed, two of which seem to have been compiled in England. The first is,—" The Elgon (Elgin) Wonder. Being a very strange, but true relation, how one Mr John Gardner, minister, near to Elgon of Murray, in the north of Scotand, fell into a trance on the 10th January, 1717, and lay as if dead, to the sight and appearance of all spectators, for the space of two days; and being put in a coffin and carry'd to his parish church, in order to be bury'd in the church-yard, and when going to put him in his grave, he was heard to make a noise in the coffin, and it being opened, he was found alive, to the wonderful astonishment of all there present; being carry'd home, and put in a warm bed, he in a little time coming to himself, related many strange and amazing things which he had seen in the other world. Also his last Sermon, preached by him after his recovery. 12mo. Printed in the year 1717."

"Scotland's Timely Remembrance, or Warnings from Heaven to vile Sinners on Earth. Being an Account of the holy Life of Mr Richard Brightly, Minister of the Gospel near Salcraig, in the South of Scotland, and of his dayly walking with God;

how at several times he heard heavenly musick when at prayer, and of many persons that appeared unto him in white raiment; also how, on the 9th of August, at night, as he was praying, he fell into a trance, and saw the state of the damned in everlasting torment, and that of the blessed in glory; and being then warned of his death by an angel, he afterwards ordered his coffine and grave to be made, and invited his parishioners to hear his last sermon, which he preached the Sunday following, having his coffine before him, and then declared his visions; and how he saw Death riding in triumph on a pale horse, of the message he had given him to warn the inhabitants of the earth of the wrath to come, and of his dying in the pulpit when he had delivered the same; lastly, of his burial, and of the harmonious musick that was heard in the air during his enterment.

"We, whose names are after-mentioned, do certifie the within printed relation to be true, and desire that the same may be published to the world. Printed in the year 1717."

This seems decidedly an English forgery. Brightly saw the New Jerusalem, of which the 12 gates were 12 pearls, and the streets pure gold.

"He dropt down in the pulpit, which caused the people to give a great outcry. They fetcht him down and laid him in a coffin. It would have made the hardest heart to shed a tear, to see the lamentation that was made for this holy man. He was a comely corp, and died with the resemblance of joy in his face.

"The names of the certifiers are,

  Sir William Parsons.
  Thomas Lestrange.
  Richard Moreton, Minister.
  Thomas Rives, Minister.
  Peter Laplasset.
  Richard Jones."

"A Wonderful Vision or Prophecie which was revealed to William Rutherford, Farmer in the Shire of the Merse, near Dunce, upon the 19th of March, 1719. With a Description of what shall befall Great Britain, especially Scotland; wherein is an Account of the wonderful Things that shall come upon Scotland, viz. such as great wars, famine, and death, and people of a strange languish shall be froges throughout our whole land; with several signs and tokens before the accomplishment of these things; all which was revealed to William Rutherford, farmer in the Merce, by an angel which appeared unto him as he was praying in his corn-yard, who opened up to him strange visions unknown to the inhabitants of the earth, with the dreadful wrath that is coming on Britain, with an eclipse of the gospel, and the great death that shall befall many, who shall be suddenly snatcht away before these things come to pass; also the glorious deliverance the church will get after these sad times are over; with the great plenty that will follow immediately thereafter, with the conversion of the heathen nations. Meal sold for four shillings per boll. The truth of this vision is attested by the minister of the parish, and four honest men, who were eye and ear-witness. Edinburgh, printed at the foot of the Horse Wynd."

Rutherford, being a very pious man, was at prayer one evening in his own corn-yard, when, at 45 minutes past seven, an angel appeared to him, and desired that he would summon the minister of the parish, and four honest men, namely, Mr John Lamb, heritor; Robert Anderson, church-elder; Alexander Cock, farmer; and William Dove, cordiner, to be present at his revelations, that the world might have nothing to object to the truth of his appearance. The minister, (Mr James Smith) and the rest, came accordingly. The minister politely invited the angel to go into a house, but he would not, and proceeded to reveal what is set forth in the title-page. After which he ascended in the clouds, to their great amazement.

The only other pamphlet to be mentioned as worthy of notice, is " A Wonderful and True Account of the Laird of Cool's Ghost," which has gone through many editions. Mr Maxwell of Cool died in the year 1724, and shortly afterwards his restless spirit appeared several times, and to sundry persons; among whom Mr Ogilvie, minister of the gospel at Innerwick, had some long conversations with it, which he committed to paper. These were published after Ogilvie's death, out of malice, or to promote laughter. Indeed, it has been said that the whole affair was a sham; be that as it may, Mrs Elizabeth Stewart of Coltness, who had entered into an epistolary correspondence on the subject with Mrs Hogg Ogilvie's daughter, seriously composed, " Remarks and Illustrations on the Narrative of Cool's Ghost," which were printed after the good lady's decease, in the year 1808; in all human probability, the last pamphlet of such a nature that ever will be sent to the Scottish press,—for chanticleer and the rising day are superseded by good sense and widely-diffused information, which have driven our ghosts to a few remote castles in the north of Scotland, where they are almost as forgotten as in the Red Sea; and our witches, though they once, according to Lindsay, could muster around their prototype of Endor, in numerous groups, from

"Athole and Argyle,
And from the Rynnis of Galloway,
With mony wofull walloway,"

Are now dwindled down into a very few old women, deemed *unluckie* by their lowly neighbours, more from having been born with what is termed *an evil eye*, than from any formal compact with the arch enemy of mankind.

APPENDIX.

NOTE 1.

THE CONVEYANCE OF INDIVIDUALS THROUGH THE AIR BY WITCHCRAFT.
Page 56.

Though the author of the pamphlet yields no belief to the anecdote of the pedlar, the wooden cut which embellishes his work exhibits the figure of a man asleep in a cellar, with others banquetting in the back ground. *Vide* frontispiece. In Aubrey's Miscellanies is a story of an ancestor of the Lord Duffus, who was suddenly transported through the air from Scotland to Paris, where he found himself in the French King's cellar, with a silver cup in his hand. In the year 1695, this cup was still in the possession of the family. See Lord Fountainhall's Decisions, vol, i. p. 15, for a curious account of the rencounter, as he calls it, betwixt Mr David Williamson, schoolmaster at Couper, and the Rosicrucians, who could make their spirits bring "noble Greek wine from the Pope's cellars" to Couper, and feasted the schoolmaster at London "with all the varieties of delicate meats, where they were all served by spirits." The truth of this story Lord Fountainhall had from Williamson's son, minister of Kirkaldie, who denied the very unsavoury conclusion with which report had defiled the banquet.

NOTE 2.
THE MARKS OF A WITCH.
Page 57.

"There have been many found in whom such characters have concurred, as by the observation of all ages and nations, are symptoms of a witch; particularly the witch's marks, *mala fama*, inability to shed tears, etc., all of them providential discoveries of so dark a crime, and which, like avenues, lead us to the secret of it. 'Tis true, one man, through the concurrence of corrosive humours, may have an insensible mark, another may be enviously defamed, and a third, through sudden grief or melancholy, not be able to weep. One or other of these may concurr in the innocent, but none do attest that all of them have concurred in any one person but a witch; and 'tis reasonable to think that these indicia taking place in witches through all places in the world, do proceed from a common cause, rather than a peculiar humour. 'Tis but rational to think that the devil, aping God, should imprint a sacrament of his covenant; and it is thought by many, of greatest repute in the learned world, that whatsoever way, whether by accident or otherwise, such insensible marks be in the body, yet no such mark as theirs, every circumstance considered, is to be found with any other but themselves. I need not insist much in describing this mark, which is sometimes like a little teate, sometimes but a blewish spot; and I myself have seen it in the body of a confessing witch, like a little powder-mark, of a blea colour, somewhat hard, and withall insensible, so as it did not bleed when I pricked it."—*A Discourse of Witchcraft, by Mr John Bell, Minister of the Gospel at Gladsmuir,* 1705, *MS.*

In another printed Tract, by the same author, entitled, "The Trial of Witchcraft; or Witchcraft Arraigned and Condemned, in some Answers to a few Questions anent Witches and Witchcraft, wherein is shewed how to know if one be a Witch, as also when one is bewitched: With some Observations upon the Witch's Mark, their compact with the Devil, the White Witches, &c."—he says, "The witch mark is sometimes like a blew spot, or a little tate, or reid spots, like flea biting; sometimes also the flesh is sunk in, and hallow, and this is put in secret places, as among the hair of the head, or eye-brows, within the lips, under the arm-pits, and even in the most secret parts of the body." Mr Robert Kirk, minister at Aberfoill, in his Secret Commonwealth, describes the witch's mark—" A spot that I have seen, as a small mole, horny, and brown-coloured; throw which mark, when a large brass pin was thrust, (both in buttock, nose, and rooff of the mouth,) till it bowed and became crooked, the witches, both men and women, nather felt a pain nor did bleed, nor knew the precise time when this was doing to them, (their eyes only being covered.")—See also Law's Memorialls, p 130, note.

NOTE 3.
SICKNESS LAID BENEATH A BARN DOOR.
Page 98.

"Answers, this article is both improbable and impossible, because it is offered to be proven, that two years interveaned between the sicknesses. Its a strange senselessness in the dittay to say that sickness should be laid beneath a barne-door, seeing sickness cannot be inherent in anything save a living creature. There is a like fable reported in Ariosto. As to the dancing of the firlot, it's certain that it was a distemperator in the subject, *id est*, in the person's brain that saw it, for he was mad. As to the mark on the lintell, denies onie sic mark; as to his death, offers to prove that he was cured by John Purves, chirurgeon, lived eleven years after, and had children."

NOTE 4.
ON BURYING AND BURNING ANIMALS ALIVE.
Page 99.

In a Dialogue concerning Witches and Witchcrafts, by George Giffard, minister of God's word at Maldon, 1603, is a story of a witch who employed an imp in the shape of a cat to destroy three hogs and a cow belonging to a farmer whom she hated.—" The man suspecting, burnt a pig alive, and, as she sayd, her cat would never go thither any more." By the way, it does not seem to have been so much the custom of the devil to give imps (or *puckrels*, as they are called in this book,) to his northern as to his English subjects. In the same black-letter Dialogue, one of the speakers says,—" I was of another jurie since, and there was a woman indicted for a witch, but not for killing any man or childe. There came in five or six against her; the first was an old woman, and she sayd she had displeased her, as she thought; and within two or three nights after, as she sate by her fire, there was a thing like a toade, or like some little crabbe-fish, which did creepe upon the harth; she tooke a beesome and swept it away, and suddenly her bodie was griped. Another fel out with her, as she said, and her hennes began to die up, untill she burnt one hen alive. A third man came in, and he said she was once angrie with him; he had a dun cow which was tyed up in a house, for it was in winter; he feared that some evil would follow, and, for his life, he could not come in where she was, but he must needs take up her tayle, and kisse under it. Two or three others came in, and said she was, by common fame, accounted a witch. We found her guiltie, and she was condemned to prison, and to the pillorie, but stood stiffe in it that she was no witch."

NOTE 5.
PECULIAR CAPS OF THE SEVENTEENTH CENTURY.
Page 116.

In Giffard's Dialogue concerning Witches and Witchcrafts, 1603, is a story of a woman who repaired to a *cunning man*, suspecting that her husband had died of witchery through the incantations of a neighbour. "He showed her the woman as plaine in a glass as we see one another, and in the very apparell she went in at that houre; for she wore an old red cap, with corners, such as women were wont to weare, and in that she appeared in the glasse." These caps remind one of that used, during his studies, by Prynne, who, according to Aubrey, "was of a strange saturnine complexion. Sir C. W. sayd once, that he had the countenance of a witch. He wore a long quilt cap, which came two or three inches at least over his eies, which served him as an umbrella to defend his eies from the light."— *Lives of Eminent Men*, p. 508.

NOTE 6.
LORD HOLLAND'S DAUGHTERS.
Page 125.

In the possession of Lord Breadalbane, is a full-length portrait of Lady Isabella, holding a lute, for her performance on which she is so much extolled by Waller. Aubrey, in his Life of Dr Kettle, President of Trinity College, Oxford, says, that during the civil war, "our grove was the Daphne for the ladies and their gallants to walke in, and many times my Lady Isabella Thynne (she lay at Balliol College) would make her entreys with a theorbo or lute played before her. I have heard her play on it in the grove myself, which she did rarely; for which Mr Edm. Waller hath, in his poems, for ever made her famous. One may say of her, as Tacitus said of Agrippina,—*Cuncta alia illæ adfuere, præter animum honestum.* She was most beautifull, most humble, charitable, &c.; but she could not subdue one thing. I remember one time this lady, and fine Mrs Fenshawe, her great and intimate friend, who lay at our college, (she was wont, and my Lady Thynne, to come to our chapell, mornings, half-dressed, like angells) would have a frolick to make a visit to the president. The old doctor quickly perceived that they came to abuse him; he addressed his discourse to Mrs

Fenshawe, saying, "Madam, your husband and father I bred up here, and I knew your grandfather; I know you to be a gentlewoman, I will not say you are a w——; but gett you gone for a very woman." At the conclusion of *Beaumont's Treatise of Spirits*, is a very remarkable account of the death of a young lady, communicated by the Bishop of Gloucester, which may properly be added to this notice respecting the daughters of Lord Holland. "Sir Charles Lee, by his first lady, had only one daughter, of which she died in child-birth; and when she was dead, her sister, the Lady Everard, desired to have the education of the child, and she was by her very well educated till she was marriageable, and a match was concluded for her with Sir William Perkins, but was then prevented in an extraordinary manner. Upon a Thursday night, she, thinking she saw a light in her chamber after she was in bed, knocked for her maid, who presently came to her; and she asked, 'why she left a candle burning in her chamber?' The maid said, she 'left none, and there was none but what she brought with her at that time;' then she said it was the fire, but that her maid told her was quite out; and said she believed it was only a dream, whereupon she said it might be so, and composed herself again to sleep; but about two of the clock she was awakened again, and saw the apparition of a little woman between her curtain and her pillow, who told her she was her mother, that she was happy, and that by twelve of the clock that day she should be with her; whereupon she knocked again for her maid, called for her clothes, and when she was dressed, went into her closet, and came not out again till nine, and then brought out with her a letter sealed to her father; brought it to her aunt, the Lady Everard, told her what had happened, and declared that as soon as she was dead, it might be sent to him; but the lady thought she was suddenly fallen mad, and thereupon sent presently away to Chelmsford for a physician and surgeon, who both came immediately; but the physician could discern no indication of what the lady imagined, or of any indisposition of her body; notwithstanding, the lady would needs have her let blood, which was done accordingly; and when the young woman had patiently let them do what they would with her, she desired that the chaplain might be called to read prayers; and when prayers were ended, she took her gittar and psalm-book, and sate down upon a chair without arms, and played and sung so melodiously and admirably, that her musick-master, who was then there, admired at it. And near the stroke of twelve, she rose and sate herself down in a great chaire with arms, and presently fetching a strong breathing or two, immediately expired, and was so suddenly cold, as was much wondered at by the physician and surgeon. She died at Waltham, in Essex, three miles from Chelmsford, and the letter was sent to Sir Charles, at his house in Warwickshire; but he was so afflicted with the death of his daughter, that he came not till she was buried; but when he came, he caused her to be taken up, and to be buried with her mother at Edminton, as she desired in her letter. This was about the year 1662, or 63; and this relation the Lord Bishop of Gloucester had from Sir Charles himself.

NOTE 7.
ON DEVILISH CHARMS.
Page 140.

"Guard against devilish charms for men and beasts, which are the very rudiments of witchcraft, and introductory to a formal and more explicit covenant with the devil. O! do not play upon the brink of the pit, least yow tumble in. There are many sorceries practised in our day, against which I would on this occasion bear my testimony, and do therefore seriously ask you, What is it you mean by your observation of times and— seasons as lucky or unlucky? What mean you by your spells, verses, words so often repeated, said fasting, or going backward? How mean yow to have success by carrying about with yow certain herbs, plants, and branches of trees? Why is it, that, fearing certain events, yow do use such superstitious means to prevent them, by laying bits of timber at doors, carrying a Bible merely for a charm, without any further use of it? What intend ye by opposing witchcraft to witchcraft, in such sort, when ye suppose one to be bewitched, ye endeavour his relief by burnings, bottles, horse-shoes, and such like magical ceremonies? How think ye to have secrets revealed unto yow, and your doubts resolved, and your minds informed, by turning a sieve or a key? Or to discover, by basons and glasses, how yow shall be related before yow die? Or do yow think to escape the guilt of sorcery, who let your Bible fall open, on purpose to determine what the state of your soul is, by the first word ye light upon?"—*A Discourse of Witchcraft, by Mr John Bell, Minister of the Gospel at Gladsmuir*, 1705, MS.

NOTE 8.
FAMILIAR SPIRITS.
Page 142.

Beaumont, in his Account of Genii, or Familiar Spirits, gives a very accurate description of two, which, he says, constantly attended himself. "They appeared both in women's habit, being of a brown complexion, and about three feet in stature; they had both black loose net-work gowns, tied with a black sash about their middles; and within the net-work appeared a gown of a golden colour, with somewhat of a light striking through it; their heads were not drest with top-knots, but they had white linnen caps on, with lace on them about three fingers breadth, and over it they had a black loose net-work hood." See also Baxter's Worlds of Spirits, p. 178, for an account of one Major Wilkie, "a Scottish soldier, and a scholar of considerable learning; he would drink too much, and had the signs of a heated brain, but no failing of his reason perceivable," who confidently affirmed, that he continually saw good and evil spirits about him, and that he had a good genius and an enemy.

NOTE 9.
FEMALES IN MASCULINE ATTIRE.
Page 147.

Prynne, in his Hidden Works of Darkness, mentions a like indiscretion committed during the reign of King Charles the First, but the lady was of a less noble extract:—"No lesse was his (the Pope's) pride puft up, when Sir William Hamilton, brother to the Earl of Abercorne, and cousen to the Marquesse Hamilton, was sent ambassadour from our queen to that court (of Rome) whose carriage was like to that of

Signior Georgio's here, carrying, clothed in man's apparell, through England, Scotland, France, and Italy, his sweetheart, Eugenius Bonny, a daughter of the yeoman of his majesties wine cellar."

THE DUKE OF LAUDERDALE ON WITCHCRAFT.

BAXTER'S "World of Spirits" having become scarce, the Author is tempted to reprint, as a proper addition to the foregoing Notice, the Sixth Chapter, which Richard entitles,—" Instances sent me from the Duke of Lauderdale; more in other Letters of his I gave away, and some Books of Forreign Wonders he sent me."

SIR,

It is sad that the Sadducean, or rather atheistical denying of spirits, or their apparitions, should so far prevail; and sadder, that the clear testimonies of so many ancient and modern authors should not convince them. But why should I wonder, if those who believe not Moses and the prophets, will not believe though one should rise from the dead? One great cause of the hardening of these infidels is, the frequent impostures which the Romanists obtrude on the world in their exorcisms and pretended miracles. Another is the too great credulity of some who make everything witchcraft which they do not understand; and a third may be the ignorance of some judges and juries, who condemn silly melancholy people upon their own confession, and perhaps slender proofs. None of these three can be denied, but it is impertinent arguing to conclude, that because there have been cheats in the world, because there are some too credulous, and some have been put to death for witches, and were not, therefore all men are deceived. There is so much written, both at home and abroad, so convincingly, and by so unquestionable authors, that I have not the vanity to add any thing, especially to you; but because you have desired me to tell you the story of the nuns at Loudun, and some others, I shall first tell you of a real possession near the place I was born in; next of disquietings by spirits, (both of which I had from unquestionable testimonies) and then I shall tell you what I saw at Loudun, concerning that which I do not doubt to call a pretended possession, sure I am a cheat. About 30 years ago, when I was a boy at school, there was a poor woman generally believed to be really possessed. She lived near the town of Duns, in the Mers, and Mr John Weems, then minister of Duns, (a man known by his works to be a learned man, and I knew him to be a godly honest man,) was perswaded she was possessed. I have heard him many times speak with my father about it, and both of them concluded it a real possession. Mr Weems visited her often, and being convinced of the truth of the thing, he, with some neighbour ministers, applied themselves to the king's privy council for a warrant to keep days of humiliation for her; but the bishops being then in power, would not allow any fasts to be kept. I will not trouble you with many circumstances; one I shall only tell you, which I think will evince a real possession. The report being spread in the country, a knight of the name of Forbes, who lived in the north of Scotland, being come to Edinborough, meeting there with a minister of the north, and both of them desirous to see the woman, the northern minister invited the knight to my father's house, (which was within ten or twelve miles of the woman) whither they came, and next morning went to see the woman. They found her a poor ignorant creature, and seeing nothing extraordinary, the minister says in Latin to the knight, "*Nondum audivimus spiritum loquentem.*" Presently a voice comes out of the woman's mouth, "*Audis loquentem, audis loquentem.*" This put the minister into some amazement, (which I think made him not mind his own Latin,) he took off his hat, and said, "*Misereatur Deus peccatoris;*" the voice presently out of the woman's mouth said, "*Dic peccatricis, dic peccatricis;*" whereupon both of them came out of the house fully satisfied, took horse immediately, and returned to my father's house at Thirlestoane Castle, in Lauderdale, where they related this passage. This I do exactly remember. Many more particulars might be got in that country, but this Latin criticism, in a most illiterate ignorant woman, where there was no pretence to dispossessing, is evidence enough, I think.

Within these 30 or 40 years, there was an unquestionable possession in the United Provinces; a wench that spoke all languages, of which I have heard many particulars when I lived in the Low Countries. But that being forreign, I will not insist on it.

As to houses disquieted with noises, I shall tell you one that happened since I was a married man, and hint at more, which, if you please, I can get you authentically attested.

Within four miles of Edenborough, there lived an aged godly minister, one that was esteemed a Puritan; his son, now minister of the same place, and then ordained his assistant. Their house was extraordinarily troubled with noises, which they and their family, and many neighbours (who for divers weeks used to go watch with them) did ordinarily hear. It troubled them most on the Saturday night, and the night before their weekly lecture day. Sometimes they would hear all the locks of the house, on doors and chests, to fly open; yea, their cloaths, which were at night locked up into trunks and chests, they found in the morning all hanging about the walls. Once they found their best linnen taken out, the table covered with it, napkins as if they had been used, yea, and liquor in their cups as if company had been there at meat. The rumbling was extraordinary; the good old man commonly called his family to prayer when it was most troublesome, and immediately it was converted into gentle knocking, like the modest knock of a finger; but as soon as prayer was done, they should hear excessive knocking, a if as beam had been heaved by strength of many men against the floor. Never was there voice or apparition; but one thing was remarkable (you must know that it is ordinary in Scotland to have a half cannon-bullet in the chimney-corner, on which they break their great coals,) a merry maid in the house, being accustomed to the rumblings, and so her fear gone, told her fellow maid-servant that if the devil troubled them that night, she would brain him, so she took the half cannon-bullet into bed; the noise did not fail to awake her, nor did she fail in her design, but took up the great bullet, and with a threatning, threw it, as she thought, on the floor, but the bullet was never more seen; the minister turned her away for meddling and talking to it. All these particulars I have had from the mouth of the minister, now living; he is an honest man, of good natural parts, well bred both in learning and by travel into foreign parts in his youth. I was not in the country myself during the time, but I have it from many other witnesses; and my father's steward lived then in a house of mine, within a mile of the place, and sent his servants constantly thither; his son now serves me, who knows it.

I could tell you an ancienter story before my time, in the house of one Burnet, in the north of Scotland, where strange things were seen, which I can get sufficiently attested. Also in the southwest border of Scotland, in Annandale, there is a house called Powdine, belonging to a gentleman called Johnston; that house hath been haunted these 50 or 60 years. At my coming to Worcester, 1651, I spoke with the gentleman, (being myself quartered within two miles of the house,) he told me many extraordinary relations consisting in his own knowledge; and I carried him to my master, to whom he made the same relations,—noises and apparitions, drums and trumpets heard before the last war yea, he said that some English soldiers quartered in his house were soundly beaten by that then irresistible inhabitant; (this last I wondered at, for I rather expected he should have been a remonstrater, and opposed the resistance,) and within this fortnight Mr James Sharp was with me, (him you know, and he is now at London,) he tells me that spirit now speaks, and appears frequently in the shape of a naked arm; but other discourses took me off from further inquiry. These things I tell you in obedience to your desire, but as I said before, I desire them not to be printed. Atheists are not to be convinced by stories; their own senses will no more convert them than sense will convert a papist from transubstantiation; and Scottish stories would make the disaffected jeer Scotland, which is the object of scorn enough already.

When I was in Dorsetshire, prisoner, one Mr Jo. Hodder, minister of Hauke-church, in that county, told me of strange apparitions and unquestionable evidences of the actings of spirits in a house, yea, a religious house of that county, of which he was himself an ear and eye-witness.

In Dorchester, also, the son of a Reverend Mr Jo. White, (who was assessor to the Assembly at Westminster,) told me many particulars of that house in Lambeth where his father lived in the time of the Assembly, which then was unquestionably haunted with spirits. I do well remember I dined with old Mr White there one day, and at dinner he told me much of it; and that that morning the spirit called up the maid to lay the beef to the fire. Of the two last you may be satisfied when you please: and at this present I am told that there is a house at Folie-John-Park, not three miles from the place, haunted with spirits.

But I must leave room for my Loudun nuns, and not write a book. In the year 1637, being at Paris in the spring, the city was so full of the possession of a whole cloyster of nuns, and some laick wenches at Loudun, books printed, and strange stories told, that few doubted it; and I, who was perswaded such a thing might be, and that it was not impossible the devil could possess a nun as well as another, doubted it as little as any body. So coming into that country, I went a day's journey out of my way to satisfy my curiosity. Into the chappel I came in the morning of a holy day, and with as little prejudice as any could have, for I believed verily to have seen some strange sights; but when I had seen exorcising enough of three or four of them in the chappel, and could hear nothing but wanton wenches singing baudy songs in French, I began to suspect a fourbe, and in great gravity went to a jesuite, and told him I had come a great way in

hope to see some strange thing, and was sorry to
be disappointed. He commended my holy
curiosity, and after he had thought a while, he
desired me to go to the Castle, and from thence,
at such an hour, to the parish church, and I
should be satisfied. I wondered at his correspondence, yet gravely went where he directed
me. In the Castle I saw little, but in the parish
church I saw a great many people gazing, and a
wench pretty well taught to play tricks yet nothing so much as I have seen twenty tumblers
and rope-dancers do. Back I came to the nuns
chappel, where I saw the jesuits still hard at
work, at several altars, and one poor capuchin,
who was an object of pity, for he was possessed
indeed with a melancholy fancy that devils were
running about his head, and constantly was
applying relicks. I saw the mother superior
exorcised, and saw the hand on which they would
have made us believe the names I. H. S. Maria
Joseph were written by miracles; (but it was
apparent to me it was done with aquafortis)
then my patience was quite spent, and I went to
a jesuit and told him my mind freely. He still
maintained a real possession, and I desired for a
tryal, to speak a strange language. He asked,
"What language?" I told him, "I would not
tell; but neither he nor all those devils should
understand me." He asked, "If I would be con-

verted upon the tryal?" (for I had discovered I was no papist.) I told him, "That was not the question, nor could all the devils in hell pervert me; but the question was, if that was a real possession, and if any could understand me, I shall confess it under my hand." His answer was, "These devils have not travelled;" and this I replyed to with a loud laughter, nor could I get any more satisfaction; only in the town I heard enough that it was a cheat invented to burn a curate, (his name, as I take it, was Cupiff,) and the man had been really burned to ashes as a witch, but the people said it was for his conversion from them. At my coming to Saumar next day, my countryman, Dr Duncan, Principal of the College at Saumar, told me how he had made a clearer discovery of the cheat in presence of the Bishop of Poitiers, and of all the country, how he had held fast one of the pretended possessed nuns arms, in spite of all the power of their exorcisms, and challenged all the devils in hell to take it out of his hand. This, with many more circumstances, he told me, and he printed them to the world; but this is already too tedious. One more journey I made to see possessed women exorcised near Antwerp, anno 1649; but saw only some great Holland wenches hear exorcism patiently, and belch most abominably. So if those were devils, they were windy devils, but I thought they were only possessed with a morning's draught of too new beer. Some of the Loudun nuns, after great resistance and squeeking, did, on great importunity, adore their host, and the jesuites did desire us to see the power of the church, where all I wondered at was his blasphemy, in saying to the pretended devil, —" *Prostratum adorabis creatorem tuum, quem digitis teneo;* " but my paper, as well as my discretion, calls for an end. Your desire, and my obedience, is all I can plead for your receiving so long a rabble, from, Sir,

Your most faithful Friend and Servant,

LAUDERDAILE.

Windsor Castle, March 12, 1659.

SINGULAR AND LAUGHABLE ACCOUNT OF THE DOINGS OF A SPIRIT IN KIRKCUDBRIGHTSHIRE.

THE following very singular and laughable Relation is reprinted, as a proper Appendix to Law's Memorials, from the original quarto pamphlet, now become scarce, though, in the first year of its appearance, it went through two editions in Scotland, and also came out in London, with many alterations as to style, printed for Andrew

Bell, at the sign of the Cross Keys in the Poultry. —Of the Author, Mr Telfair, the Editor has only discovered that, in the year 1687, he was chaplain to Sir Thomas Kirkpatrick of Closeburne, Bart., whose Diary contains this notice respecting him:—"*Item*, William Forest and George Jonstone entered to my service at Whitsunday last, 1687; the one to carry the boys, and be butler; the other, George Jonstone, to serve my sone; and they have offered themselves to my good will for half a year's tryall of their service. —*Item*, Mr Alexander Tailfer entered at the said term to serve as chaipline, and he is to have yearlie an hundreth merks."—As Sir Thomas was of the Episcopal persuasion, it is to be supposed that Mr Alexander then professed the same creed; but he found it convenient, like several of his brethren, to change his mind on the fiery ordeal of the Revolution.

A True Relation of an Apparition, Expressions, and Actings, of a Spirit, which infested the House of Andrew Mackie, in Ring-Croft of Stocking, in the Paroch of Rerrick, in the Stewarty of Kirkcudbright, in Scotland, 1695. By Mr Alexander Telfair, Minister of that Paroch; and attested by many other Persons, who were also Eye and Eur Witnesses.

Eph. vi. 11. Put on the whole armour of God, that ye may be able to stand against the wiles of the Devil.—Vers. 12. For we wrestle not against flesh and blood, but against principalities, and powers, &c.—James iv. 7. Resist the Devil, and he will flee from you.

Edinburgh: Printed by George Mosman, and are to be sold at his Shop in the Parliament Closs. 1696.

At Edinburgh, the 7th of January, 1696.

THE Lords of his Majesty Privy-Council do hereby allow George Mosman, stationer in Edinburgh, to print, vend, and sell a book, entituled A True Relation of an Apparition, Expressions, and Actings of a Spirit, which infested the house of Andrew Mackie, in Ring-Croft of Stocking, in the Paroch of Rerrick, in the Stewarty of Kirkcudbright; and discharges any other persons whatsoever to imprint, vend, or sell the said book, for the space of one year after the date hereof, except the said George Mosman and his assegneys, under the penaltie of having the said books confiscate to the use of the said George Mosman, and of paying to him the sum of Fourty Pounds Scots for each transgression, besides the forsaid confiscation *toties quoties.* Extracted by me,

GIL. ELIOT, *Cls. Sci. Cons.*

TO THE READER.

I ASSURE you it is contrare to my genius, (all circumstances being considered,) to appear in print to the view of the world, yet these motives have prevailed with me to publish the following

Relation, (beside the satisfying of some reverend brethren in the ministry, and several worthy Christians) :—As, 1. The conviction and confutation of that prevailing spirit of atheism and infidelity in our time, denying, both in opinion and practice, the existence of spirits, either of God or Devils; and consequently a Heaven and Hell; and imputing the voices, apparitions, and actings of good or evil spirits to the melancholick disturbance or distemper of the brains and fancies of those who pretend to hear, see, or feel them. 2. To give occasion to all who read this, to bless the Lord, who hath sent a stronger (even Christ Jesus) than the strong man, to bind him and spoil him of his goods, and to destroy the works of the Devil; and even by these things whereby Satan thinks to propagate his kingdom of darkness, to discover, weaken, and bring it down. 3. To induce all persons, particularly masters of families, to private and family prayer, lest the neglect of it provoke the Lord, not only to pour out his wrath upon them otherwise, but to let Satan loose to haunt their persons and families with audible voices, apparitions, and hurt to their persons and goods. 4. That ministers and congregations, where the gospel is in any measure in purity and power, may be upon their guard to wrestle, according to the word of God, against these principalities and powers, and spiritual wickednesses, who still seek to marr the success and fruit of the gospel, sometimes by force, and sometimes by fraud, sometimes secretly, and sometimes openly, (*tunc tua res agitur, paries cum proximus ardet*); and for these ends learn to know his wiles, and put on the whole armour of God, that they may be able to debate with him. And, 5. That all who are by the goodness of God free from these audible voices, apparitions, or hurts from Satan, may learn to ascribe praise and glory to God, who leads them not into temptation, but delivers them from evil; and that this true and attested account of Satan's methods in this place may carry the forsaid ends, is the earnest prayer of an weak labourer in the work of the gospel in that place, and your servant for Christ's sake,

ALEXANDER TELFAIR.

Edinburgh, Decer. 21, 1695.

A True Relation of an Apparition, Expressions, and Actings of a Spirit, which infested the House of Andrew Mackie, in Ring-Croft of Stocking, in the Paroch of Rerrick, in the Stewarty of Kirkcudbright, in Scotland.

WHEREAS many are desirous to know the truth of the matter, as to the evil spirit and its actings, that troubleth the family of Andrew Mackie, in Ring-Croft of Stocking, &c., and are lyable to be mis-informed, as I do find by the reports that come to my own ears of that matter; therefore, that satisfaction may be given, and such mistakes may be cured or prevented, I, the minister of the said paroch, (who was present several times, and was witness to many of its actings, and have heard an account of the whole of its methods and actings from the persons present, towards whom, and before whom it did act), have given the ensuing and short account of the whole matter, which I can attest to be the very truth as to that affair; and before I come to the Relation itself, I premise these things with respect to what might have been the occasion and rise of that spirit's appearing and acting.

1. The said Andrew Mackie being a meason to his employment, 'tis given out, that when he took the meason-word, he devouted his first child to the Devil; but I am certainly informed he never took the same, and knows not what that word is. He is outwardly moral; there is nothing known to his life and conversation, but honest, civil, and harmless, beyond many of his neighbours; doth delight in the company of the best; and when he was under the trouble of that evil spirit, did pray to the great satisfaction of many. As for his wife and children, none have imputed any thing to them as the rise of it, nor is there any ground, for ought I know, for any to do so.

2. Whereas its given out that a woman, *sub malâ famâ*, did leave some cloaths in that house, in the custody of the said Andrew Mackie, and died before they were given up to her, and he or his wife should have keeped some of them back from her friends. I did seriously pose both him and his wife upon the matter; they declared they knew not what things were left, being bound up in a sack, but did deliver entirely to her freinds all they received from the woman, which I am apt to believe.

3. Whereas one   Macknaught, who sometimes before possessed that house, did not thrive in his own person or goods. It seems he had sent his son to a witch-wife, who lived then at the Routing-bridge, in the paroch of Iron-gray, to enquire what might be the cause of the decay of his person and goods. The youth, meeting with some forreign souldiers, went abroad to Flanders, and did not return with an answer. Some years after, there was one John Redick in this paroch, who, having had occasion to go abroad, met with the said young Macknaught in Flanders, and they knowing other, Macknaught enquired after his father and other friends; and finding the said John Redick was to go home, desired him to go to his father, or who ever dwelt in the Ring-croft, and desire them to raise the door-threshold, and search till they found a

tooth, and burn it, for none who dwelt in that house would thrive till that was done. The said John Redick coming home, and finding the old man Macknaught dead, and his wife out of that place, did never mention the matter, nor further mind it, till this trouble was in Andrew Mackie's family, then he spoke of it, and told the matter to myself. Betwixt Macknaught's death, and Andrew Mackie's possession of this house, there was one Thomas Telfair, who possest it some years; what way he heard the report of what the witch-wife had said to Macknaught's son, I cannot tell; but he searched the door-threshold, and found something like a tooth; did compare it with the tooth of man, horse, nolt, and sheep, (as he said to me), but could not say which it did resemble, only it did resemble a tooth. He did cast it in the fire, where it burnt like a candle, or so much tallow; yet he never knew any trouble about that house by night or by day, before or after, during his possession. These things premised being suspected to have been the occasion of the trouble, and there being no more known as to them, than what is now declared, I do think the matter still unknown, what may have given an arise thereto. But leaving this I subjoin the matter as follows.

In the moneth of February, 1695, the said Andrew Mackie had some young beasts, which in the night-time were still loosed, and their bindings broken; he taking it to be the unrulyness of the beasts, did make stronger and stronger bindings of withes and other things; but still all were broken. At last he suspected it to be some other thing, whereupon he removed them out of that place; and the first night thereafter, one of them was bound with a hair-tedder to the balk of the house, so strait that the feet of the beast only touched the ground, but could not move no way else, yet it sustained no hurt. An other night, when the family were all sleeping, there was the full of an back-creel of peets set together in midst of the house-floor, and fire put in them; the smoak wakened the family, otherwise the house had been burnt; yet nothing all the while was either seen or heard.

Upon the 7th of March, there were stones thrown in the house in all the places of it; but it could not be discovered from whence they came, what, or who threw them. After this manner it continued till the Sabbath, now and then throwing both in the night and day; but was busiest throwing in the night-time.

Upon Saturday, the family being all without, the children coming in saw something, which they thought to be a body sitting by the fire-side with a blanket (or cloath) about it, whereat they were affraid. The youngest, being a boy about nine or ten years of age, did chide the rest, saying, why are you fear'd? let us saine (or bless) our selves, and then there is no ground to fear't. He perceived the blanket to be his, and saining (or blessing) himself, ran and pulled the blanket from it, saying, "Be what it will, it hath nothing to do with my blanket;" and then they found it to be a four footed stool set upon the end, and the blanket cast over it.

Upon the Sabbath, being the 11th of March, the crook and pot-clips were taken away, and were awanting four days, and were found at last on a loaft, where they had been sought several times before. This is attested by Charles Macklelane of Colline, and John Cairns in Hardhills. It was observed, that the stones which hit any person had not half their natural weight; and the throwing was more frequent on the Sabbath than at other times; and especially in time of prayer, above all other times, it was busiest, then throwing most at the person praying. The said Andrew Mackie told the matter to me upon Sabbath after sermon. Upon the Tuesday thereafter I went to the house, did stay a considerable time with them, and prayed twice, and there was no trouble. Then I came out with a resolution to leave the house, and as I was standing speaking to some men at the barn end, I saw two little stones drop down on the croft at a little distance from me; and then immediately some came crying out of the house, that it was become as ill as ever within; whereupon I went into the house again, and as I was at prayer, it threw several stones at me, but they did no hurt, being very small; and after there was no more trouble till the 18th day of March, and then it began as before, and threw more frequently greater stones, whose strokes were sorer where they hit; and thus it continued to the 21st. Then I went to the house, and stayed a great part of the night, but was greatly troubled; stones and several other things were thrown at me; I was struck several times on the sides and shoulders very sharply with a great staff, so that those who were present heard the noise of the strokes. That night it threw off the bed-side, and rapped upon the chists and boards, as one calling for access. This is attested by Charles Macklelane of Colline, William Mackminn, and John Tait in Torr. That night, as I was once at prayer, leaning on a bed-side, I felt something pressing up my arme; I casting my eyes thither, perceived a little white hand and arm, from the elbow down, but presently it evanished. It is to be observed, that, notwithstanding of all that was felt and heard, from the first to the last of this matter, there was never any thing seen, except that hand I saw: and a friend of the said

Andrew Mackie's said, he saw as it were a young man, red faced, with yellow hair, looking in at the window; and other two or three persons, with the said Andrew his children, saw, at several times, as it were a young boy about the age of fourteen years, with gray cloths, and a bonnet on his head, but presently disappeared; as also what the three children saw sitting by the fireside.

Upon the 22d the trouble still increased, both against the family, and against the neighbours who came to visite them, by throwing stones, and beating them with staves; so that some were forced to leave the house before their inclination. This is attested by Charles Macklelane of Colline, and Andrew Tait in Torr. Some it would have met as they came to the house, and stoned with stones about the yards, and in like manner stoned as they went from the house; of whom Thomas Telfair in Stocking was one. It made a little wound on the said Andrew Mackie's brow; did thrust several times at his shoulder, he not regarding; at last it gripped him so by the hair, that he thought something like nails of fingers scratched his skin. It dragged severals up and down the house by the cloaths. This is attested by Andrew Tait. It gripped one John Keige, miller in Auchincairn, so by the side, that he intreated his neighbours to help, and cryed it would rive the side from him. That night it lifted the cloaths off the children as they were sleeping in bed, and beat them on the hipps as if it had been with one's hand, so that all who were in the house heard it. The door-barr and other things would go thorrow the house, as if a person had been carrying them in their hand, yet nothing seen doing it. This is attested by John Telfair in Achinleck, and others. It rattled on the chests and bed-sides with a staff, and made a great noise; and thus it continued by throwing stones, stricking with staves, and rattling in the house, till the 2d of April. At night it cryed Wisht, wisht, at every sentence in the close of prayer; and it whistled so distinctly, that the dog barked, and ran to the door, as if one had been calling to hound him.

Aprile 3d, it whistled several times, and cryed Wisht, wisht. This is attested by Andrew Tait. Upon the 4th of Aprile, Charles Macklelane of Colline, landlord, with the said Andrew Mackie, went to a certain number of ministers met at Buttle, and gave them an account of the matter, whereupon these ministers made publick prayers for the family; and two of their number, viz. Mr Andrew Æwart, minister of Kells, and Mr John Murdo, minister of Corsmichael, came to the house, and spent that night in fasting and praying; but it was very cruel against them, especially by throwing great stones, some of them about half an stone weight. It wounded Mr Andrew Æwart twice in the head, to the effusion of his blood; it pulled off his wigg in time of prayer, and when he was holding out his napkin betwixt his hands, it cast a stone in the napkin, and therewith threw it from him. It gave Mr John Murdo several sore strokes, yet the wounds and bruises received did soon cure. There were none in the house that night escaped from some of its fury and cruelty. That night it threw a firie peet amongst the people; but did no hurt, it only disturbed them in time of prayer. And also in the dawning, as they rose from prayer, the stones poured down on all who were in the house to their hurt. This is attested by Mr Andrew Æwart, Mr John Murdo, Charles Macklelane, and John Tait.

Upon the 5th of Aprile, it set some thatch-straw in fire which was in the barne-yeard. At night, the house being very throng with neighbours, the stones were still thrown down among them. As the said Andrew Mackie his wife went to bring in some peets for the fire, when she came to the door she found a broad stone to shake under her foot, which she never knew to be loose before; she resolved with herself to see what was beneath it in the morning thereafter.

Upon the 6th of Aprile, when the house was

quiet, she went to the stone, and there found seven small bones, with blood, and some flesh, all closed in a piece of old suddled paper; the blood was fresh and bright. The sight whereof troubled her, and being affraid, laid all down again, and ran to Colline his house, being an quarter of an mile distant; but in that time it was worse than ever it was before, by throwing stones and fire-balls in and about the house; but the fire as it lighted did evanish. In that time it threw an hot-stone into the bed betwixt the children, which burnt through the bed-cloaths; and after it was taken out by the man's eldest son, and had lyen on the floor more nor an hour and an half, the said Charles Macklelane of Colline could not hold it in his hand for heat. This is attested be Charles Macklelane. It thrust an staff thorrow the wall of the house above the children in the bed, shook it over them, and groaned. When Colline came to the house, he went to prayer before he offered to lift the bones. All the while he was at prayer it was most cruel; but as soon as he took up the bones the trouble ceased. (This is attested be Charles Macklelane.) He sent them presently to me; upon sight whereof I went immediately to the house. While I was at prayer, it threw great stones which hitt me, but they did not hurt; then there was no more trouble that night.

The 7th Aprile, being the Sabbath, it began again and threw stones, and wounded William Macminn, a blacksmith, on the head; it cast a plough-sock at him, and also an trough-stone, upwards of three stone weight, which did fall upon his back, yet he was not hurt thereby. Attested by William Macminn. It set the house twice in fire, yet there was no hurt done, in respect some neighboures were in the house, who helped to quench it. At night in the twilight as John Mackie, the said Andrew Mackie his eldest son, was coming home, near to the house, there was an extraordinary light fell about him, and went before him to the house with a swift motion. That night it continued after its wonted manner.

Aprile 8th. In the morning as Andrew Mackie went down the closs, he found a letter both written and sealed with blood. It was directed on the back thus: 3 years tho shall haue to repent a net it well, and within was written: Wo be to the Cotlland Repent and tak warning for the door of hauen at all Redy bart against the I am sent for a warning to the to fliee to god yet troublt shallt this man be for twenty days a 3 rpent repnent opent scotland or els tow shall. In the midle of the day, the persons alive who lived in that house since it was built, being about twenty-eight years, were conveined by appointment of the civil magistrate before Colline, myself, and others, and did all touch the bones, in respect there was some suspicion of secret murder committed in the place; but nothing was found to discover the same.

Upon the 9th of Aprile, the letter and bones were sent to the ministers, who were all occasionally met at Kirkcudbright. They appointed five of their number, viz. Mr John Murdo, Mr James Monteith, Mr John Mackmillan, Mr Samuel Spalding, and Mr William Falconer, with me, to go to the house, and spend so much time in fasting and praying as we were able.

Upon the 10th of Aprile, we went to the house, and no sooner did I begin to open my mouth, but it threw stones at me, and all within the house, but still worst at him who was at duty. It came often with such force upon the house, that it made all the house shake; it brake an hole thorrow the timber and thatch of the house, and poured in great stones, one whereof, more then an quarter weight, fell upon Mr James Monteith his back, yet he was not hurt. It threw an other with great force at him when he was praying, bigger than a man's fist, which hitt him on the breast, yet he was neither hurt nor moved thereby. It was thought fit that one of our number, with an other person, should go by turnes and stand under the hole in the outside, so there was no more trouble from that place; but the barne being joyned to the end of the house, it brake down the barne-door and midwall, and threw stones up the house, but did no great hurt. It gripped and handled the legs of some, as with a man's hand; it hoised up the feet of others while standing on the ground; thus it did to William Lennox of Mill-house, myself, and others. In this manner it continued till ten a clock at night; but after that there was no more trouble while we were about the house. This is attested by Mrs James Monteith, John Murdo, Samuel Spalding, Mr Falconer, William Lennox, and John Tait. The 11th, 12th, 13th, it was worse than ever it was before, for not any who came into the house did escape heavy strocks. There was one Andrew Tait in Torr, as he was coming to stay with the familie all night, by the way his dog catched a thulmard, when he came in he cast it by in the house; thereafter there were other three young men who came in also, and when they were all at prayer the evil spirit beat them with the dead thulmard, and threw it before them. The three who knew it not to be in the house were greatly affrighted, especially one Samuel Thomson, a chapman, whom it also gripped by the side and back, and thrust as if it had been an hand beneath his cloaths, and into his pockets; he was so affrighted that he took sickness immediately. This is attested by Andrew Tait.

The 14th, being the Sabbath, it set some straw in fire that was in the barn-yeard, and threw stones while ten a clock at night; it threw an dike-spade at the said Andrew Mackie, with the mouth toward him; but he received no hurt. While an meal-sive was tossed up and down the house, the said Andrew Mackie takes hold of it, and as it were with difficulty gets the grip keeped; at last all within the rim is torn out. Thereafter it threw an handful of the sive rolled together at Thomas Robertson in Airds, who was witness to this; yet in all thir actings there was never any thing seen but what I mentioned before.

Upon the 15th Aprile, William Anderson, a drover, and James Paterson, his son-in-law, came to the house with Colline in the evening. Colline going home a while within night, the said Andrew Mackie sent his sones to convoy him; as they returned they were cruelly stoned, and the stones rolled amongst their legs, like to break them. Shortly after they came in, it wounded William Anderson on the head, to the great effusion of his blood. In time of prayer it whisled, groaned, and cryed Whisht, whisht. This is attested by John Cairnes.

The 16th, it continued whisting, groaning,

whisling, and throwing stones in time of prayer; it cryed Bo, bo, and Kick, cuck, and shoke men back and foreward, and hoised them up as if it would lift them off their knees. This is attested by Andrew Tait.

The whole family went from the house, and left five honest neighbours to wait on the same all night; but there was no hurt done to them, nor the family where they were, nor to those neighbours who stayed in the said Andrew Mackie his house; only the cattle were cast over other to the hazard of killing them, as they were bound to the stakes, and some of them were loosed. This is attested by John Cairnes.

Upon the 18th they returned to their house again, and there was no hurt done to them nor their cattle that night, except in a little house where there were some sheep; it coupled them together in paires by the neck with straw ropes, made of an bottle of straw, which it took off an loft in the stable, and carryed to the sheep-house, which is three or four pair of butts distant, and it made more ropes than it needed for binding the sheep, which it left beside the straw in the sheep-house. This is attested by Andrew Tait.

Upon the 19th it fired the straw in the barn; but Andrew Mackie put it out (being there threshing) without doing any hurt. It shot staves thorrow the wall at him, but did no hurt.

The 20th, it continued throwing stones, whisling and whisting, with all its former words. When it hit any person, and said, Take you that till you get more, that person was sure immediately of an other; but when it said, Take you that, the person got no more for a while. This is attested by John Tait.

The 21st, 22d, 23d, it contained casting stones, beating with staves, and throwing peet-mud in the faces of all in the house, especially in time of prayer, with all its former tricks.

The 24th being a day of humiliation appointed to be kept in the parish for that cause, all that day, from morning to night, it contained, in a most fearfull manner without intermission, throwing stones with such cruelty and force, that all in the house feared lest they should be killed.

The 25th, it threw stones all night, but did no great hurt.

The 26th, it threw stones in the evening, and knocked on a chist several times, as one to have access; and began to speak, and call those who were sitting in the house witches and rukes, and said it would take them to hell. The people then in the house said among themselves, if it had any to speak to it, now it would speak. In the mean time Andrew Mackie was sleeping. They wakened him, and then he hearing it say, "Thou shalt be troubled till Tuesday," asked,

"Who gave the a commission?" To whom it answered, "God gave me a commission; and I am sent to warn the land to repent; for a judgement is to come, if the land do not quickly repent, and commanded him to reveal it upon his perrill; and if the land did not repent, it said it would go to its father, and get a commission to return with an hundred worse than itself, and would trouble every particular family in the land." Andrew Mackie said to those who were with him, "If I should tell this, I would not be believed." Then it said, "Fetch betters; fetch the minister of the paroch, and two honest men upon Tuesday's night, and I shall declare before them what I have to say." Then it said, "Praise me, and I will whistle to you; worship me, and I will trouble you no more." Then Andrew Mackie said, "The Lord, who delivered the three children out of the fiery furnace, deliver me, and mine this night from the temptations of Satan." Then it replyed, "You might as well have said, Shadrah, Meshah, and Abednego." In the mean time, while Andrew Mackie was speaking, there was one James Telfair in Buttle, who was adding a word, to whom it said, "You are basely bred, meddling in other men's discourse, wherein you are not concerned." It likewise said, "Remove your goods, for I will burn the house." He answered, "The Lord stop Satan's fury, and hinder him of his designs." Then it said, "I will do it, or you shall guide well." All this is attested by John Tait in Torr, and several others who cannot subscribe.

Upon the 27th it set the house seven times in fire. The 28th being the Sabbath, from sun-rising to sun-setting, it still set the house in fire; as it was quenched in one part, instantly it was fired in an other; and in the evening, when it could not get its designs fulfilled in burning the house, it pulled down the end of the house, all the stone-work thereof, so that they could not abide in it any longer, but went and kindled their fire in the stable.

Upon the Sabbath night, it pulled one of the children out of the bed, gripping him, as he thought, by the craig and shoulders; and took up the block of a tree, as great as a plough-head, and held it above the children, saying, "If I had a commission I would brain them;" thus it expressed itself in the hearing of all who were in the house. Attested by William Mackminn and John Corsby.

The 29th being Munday, it continued setting fire in the house. The said Andrew Mackie finding the house so frequently set in fire, and being weary quenching it, he went and put out all the fire that was about the house, and poured water upon the hearth; yet after it fired the house several times, when there was no fire within an quarter of an mile of the house. This is attested by Charles Macklelane and John Cairnes. In the midest of the day, as Andrew Mackie was threshing in the barne, it whispered in the wall, and then cryed " Andrew, Andrew," but he gave no answer to it. Then with an auster, angry voice, as it were, it said, "Speak;" yet he gave no answer. Then it said, "Be not troubled, you shall have no more trouble, except some casting of stones upon the Twesday to fulfill the promise;" and said, "Take away your straw." I went to the house about eleven a clock; it fired the house once after I went there. I stayed all night till betwixt three and four in the Twesday's morning, dureing which time there was no trouble about the house, except two little stones dropped down at the fire-side, as we were sitting down at our first entry. A little after I went away, it began to throw stones as formerly. This is attested by Charles Macklelane and John Tait.

Upon Tuesday's night, being the 30th of April, Charles Macklelane of Colline, with several neighbours, were in the barne. As he was at prayer he observed a black thing in the corner of the barne, and it did increase, as if it would fill the whole house. He could not discern it to have any form, but as if it had been a black cloud; it was affrighting to them all; and then it threw bear-chaff, and other mud upon their faces; and after did grip severals who were in the house by the middle of the body, by the arms and other parts of their bodies so strait, that some said, for five days thereafter they thought they felt these gripps. After an hour or two of the night was thus past, there was no more trouble. This is attested by Charles Macklelane, Thomas Mackminn, Andrew Paline, John Cairns, and John Tait.

Upon Wednesday's night, being the 1st of May, it fired a little sheep-house; the sheep were got out safe, but the sheep-house was wholly burnt. Since there hath not been any trouble about the house by night nor by day. Now all things aforesaid being of undoubted verity, therefore I conclude with that of the Apostle, 1 Pet. v. 8, 9. "Be sober, be vigilant, because your adversary the devil, as a roaring lion, walketh about seeking whom he may devour: Whom resist, stedfast in the faith."

This Relation is attested, as to what they particularly saw, heard, and felt, by

  Mr ANDREW ÆWART, Minister at Kells.
  Mr JAMES MONTEITH, Minister at Borg.
  Mr JOHN MURDO, Minister at Corsmichael.
  Mr SAMUEL SPALDING, Minister at Partan.

Mr WILLIAM FALCONER, Minister at Keltoun.
CHARLES MACKLELANE of Colline.
WILLIAM LENNOX of Millhouse.
ANDREW TAIT in Torr.
JOHN TAIT in Torr.
JOHN CAIRNS in Hardhills.
WILLIAM MACKMINN.
JOHN CORSBY.
THOMAS MACKMINN.
ANDREW PALINE. &c.

EDITORIAL APPENDIX.

SHORT LIST OF BOOKS ON SCOTTISH WITCHCRAFT AND SUPERSTITION.

News from Scotland, declaring the damnable Life of Doctor Fian, a notable Sorcerer, who was burned at Edinbrough in January last, 1591.

    London : W. Wright (1592). Small 4to, Black Letter, Woodcut Front. Reprinted for the Roxburgh Club, 1816.

Daemonologie in forme of a Dialogue, diuided into three Bookes.

    Edin. : Printed by R. Waldegrave, 1597. Small 4to.

Daemonologie in forme of a Dialogue, written by the high and mighty Prince James, by the Grace of God King of England, Scotland, France and Ireland, Defender of the Faith, &c.

    London : By Arnold Hatfield for Robert Wald-graue, 1603. Small 4to.

Trial, Confessions and Execution of Isobel Inch, John Stewart, Margaret Barclay and Isobel Crawford For Witchcraft, at Irvine, Anno 1618.

    A. Guthrie, Printer, Ardrossan, N.D. 8vo.

Trials for Witchcraft, Sorcery, and Superstition in Orkney, 1624-1643. From "Abbotsford Club Miscellany," and issued separately, 4to.

Trial of Witches in Shetland, A.D. 1644. From Hibbert's "Description of Shetland," 1822, and issued separately, 4to.

Confessions and Trials of the Witches of Forfar, 1661, in Reliquiæ Antiquæ Scoticæ.
    Edinburgh: T. G. Stevenson. 1848.

Satan's Invisible World Discovered; or A Choice Collection of Modern relations, proving evidently against the Sadducees and Atheists of this present Age that there are Devils, Spirits, Witches and Apparitions, from Authentick Records, Attestations of Famous Witnesses and undoubted Verity. To all which is added, That Marvellous History of Major Weir and his Sister. With two Relations of Apparitions at Edinburgh. By George Sinclair, late Professor of Philosophy in the Colledge of Glasgow.
    Edinburgh: Printed by John Reid, 1685. 12mo.

This was a very popular book in Scotland, many editions were issued, the latest and best being—

Satan's Invisible World Discovered. By George Sinclair, Professor of Philosophy and Mathematics in the University of Glasgow, 1654-1696.
    Reprinted from the Original Edition Published at Edinburgh in 1685. Accompanied with a Bibliographical Notice and Supplement, &c. Edinburgh: Thomas George Stevenson, 1871. Large and small paper, Front.

Secret Commonwealth, or A Treatise displayeing the Chiefe Curiosities as they are in Use among diverse of the People of Scotland to this Day;—Singularities for the most Part peculiar to that Nation. A subject not heretofore discoursed of by any of our Writters, and yet ventured on in an Essay to suppress the impudent and growing Atheisme of this Age and to satisfie the Desire of some choice Friends. By Mr. Robert Kirk, Minister at Aberfoill, 1691.

Edinburgh : Reprinted by James Ballantyne & Co. for Longman, Hurst, Rees, Orme & Brown, Paternoster Row, London, 1815. One Hundred Copies, 4to.

A True Relation of an Apparition, Expressions and Actings of a Spirit which infested the House of Andrew Mackie in Ring-Croft of Stocking, in the Parish of Rerrick, in the Stewartry of Kirkcudbright, in Scotland. By Mr. Andrew Telfair, Minister of that Paroch, and attested by many other persons who were also eye and ear witnesses.

Edinburgh : Printed by George Mossman, and are to be sold at his Shop in the Parliament Close. 1696. Small 4to.

New Confutation of Sadducism, being a Narrative of a Spirit which infested the House of Andrew Mackie of Ring-Croft, Galloway, in 1695.

Small 4to. London, 1696.

This curious pamphlet is reprinted in Law's "Memorialls," M'Kenzie's "History of Galloway," and elsewhere.

A Relation of the Diabolical Practices of the Witches of the Sheriffdom of Renfrew in the Kingdom of Scotland, contain'd In their Tryals, Examination and Confessions. And for which several of them have been Executed this present year 1697.

London : Printed for Hugh Newman at the Grasshopper in the Poultry. Small 4to.

Narrative of the Sufferings and Relief of a Young Girl in the West (Christian Shaw, the Laird of Bargarran's Daughter), with Trial of the seven Witches condemned to be execute at Paisley.

12mo. Edinburgh : Watson, 1698.

Sadducismus Debellatus; Or, A True Narrative of the Sorceries and Witchcrafts Exercised By the Devil and his Instruments upon Mrs. Christian Shaw, Daughter of Mr. John Shaw of Bargarran, in the County of Renfrew, in the West of Scotland, from Aug., 1696, to Apr., 1697, Containing the Journal of her Sufferings, as it was Exhibited and Prov'd by the Voluntary Confession of some of the Witches and other Unexceptionable Evidence before the Commissioners Appointed by the Privy Council of Scotland to enquire into the same. Collected from the Records.

London: Printed for D. Newman and A. Ball, at the Grasshopper, in the Poultry, and at Cross Keys and Bible in Cornhill, near Stocks-Market, 1698. Small 4to.

A Narrative of the Sufferings and Relief of a Young Girl Strangely Molested by Evil Spirits and their Instruments in the West: Collected from Authentic Testimonies, with a Preface and Postscript, containing Reflections in what is most Material or Curious, either in the History or Trial of the Seven Witches who were condemned and Burnt in the Gallow-Green of Paisley.

Paisley: Printed and Sold by Alexander Weir, 1775. 12mo.

From *Authentic Documents.* A History of the Witches of Renfrewshire who were burned on the Gallowgreen of Paisley. Published by the editor of the Paisley Repository.

Paisley: Printed by J. Neilson for John Millar, Bookseller, 1809. 12mo.

A History of the Witches of Renfrewshire. A New Edition. With an Introduction, Embodying Extracts hitherto unpublished from the Records of the Presbytery of Paisley.

Paisley: Alex. Gardner, 1877. Front. Large and Small Paper.

Witchcraft Proven, Arraign'd, and Condemn'd, &c., by a Lover of the Truth.
  Glasgow, 1697. 12mo.

The author is said to be the Rev. John Bell, minister of Gladsmuir.

Relation of Witchcraft at Pittenwheam.
  Edinburgh, 1704. 8vo.

An Answer of a Letter from a Gentleman in Fife to a Nobleman containing A brief Account of the Barbarous and illegal Treatment these poor Women accused of Witchcraft met with from the Baillies of Pittenweem and others; with some few Observations thereon. To which is added An Account of the horrid and Barbarous Murder in a Letter from a Gentleman in Fife to his Friend in Edinburgh, Feb. 5th, 1705.
  Small 4to. Printed in the year 1705.

A Just Reproof to the False Reports and Unjust Calumnies in the Foregoing Letters.
  (No title-page or date.)

ΔΕΥΤΕΡΟΣΚΟΠΙΑ;
OR, A

Brief Discourse concerning the Second Sight commonly so called. By the Reverend John Frazer, Minister of Teree and Coll and Dean of the Isles. And Published by Mr. Andrew Symson, with a Short Account of the Author.
  Edinburgh: Printed by Mr. Andrew Symson, Anno Domini MDCCVII.

A Treatise on The Second Sight, Dreams, and Apparitions, with several instances sufficiently attested; and An Appendix of Others equally Authentic. The Whole Illustrated with Letters to and from the Author on the Subject of his Treatise; and A Short Dissertation on the Mischievous Effects of Loose Principles. By Theophilus Insulanus.

 Edinburgh: Printed by Ruddiman, Auld, and Co., Printers, Morocco's Close, Lawnmarket. 1763. Small 8vo.

(Reprinted along with Kirk's "Secret Commonwealth," 1815, and in Miscellanea Scotica, 4 vols.—Glasgow, 1820.)

Macleod's History of Witches. London, 1793.
 (Front and engraved title.)

The History of Witches, Ghosts, and Highland Seers.
 Berwick: R. Taylor, N.D. [1803.] 12mo. Front.

Belief in Witchcraft unsupported by Scripture. By the Rev. James Paterson.
 Aberdeen, 1815. 8vo.

A Collection of Rare and Curious Tracts on Witchcraft and the Second Sight; with an Original Essay on Witchcraft.
 Edinburgh: Printed for D. Webster, 1820. 8vo.

The Luckless Drave, Wreck of the *John and Agnes* near Dunbar, and other Poems, with Notes and Anecdotes of the Witches of East Lothian.
 Edinburgh, 1820. 12mo. Woodcuts.

Witchcraft Detected and Prevented; or the School of Black Art newly opened.

 Peterhead: Sold by Peter Buchan, 1823. 12mo Front. Several other editions later.

Representation from the Sheriff Depute of Ross to the Committee of the Privy Council anent the Witches of Kilernan, in Reliquiae Scoticae. Edited by James Maidment.

 Edinburgh: T. G. Stevenson. 1828.

Scott's Letters on Demonology and Witchcraft.

 London, 1830. 12mo.

Scott's Letters on Demonology and Witchcraft. Illustrated by George Cruikshank.

 London, 1831. 12mo.

The plates are both plain and coloured.

Numerous other editions.

The Darker Superstitions of Scotland. Illustrated from History and Practice by John Graham Dalyell, F.A.S.E.

 Edinburgh: Waugh and Innes, 1834. 8vo.

The Darker Superstitions of Scotland, by John Graham Dalyell, Esq., F.A.S.E.

 Glasgow: Printed for Richard Griffin and Co. 1835.

This is the same edition with a new title-page.

The Holocaust; or, The Witch of Monzie. A Poem, illustrative of the Cruelties of Superstition, with Notes by the Rev. George Blair.

 London, 1845. 8vo.

The Philosophy of Witchcraft. By J. Mitchell and J. N. Dickie.
    Edinburgh: Oliver & Boyd, 1840. Front. 12mo.

In addition to the foregoing list, which might have been considerably extended, those who wish to study the subject are recommended to consult Sir Geo. Mackenzie's "Laws and Customes of Scotland in Matters Criminal," Pitcairn's "Criminal Trials," Law's "Memorialls," and Woodrow's "Analecta."

INDEX.

Aberdeen, a young man infested by a spirit, 35; Disappearance of sea-gulls, 120
Adamsone, Archbishop of St. Andrews, 46
Admiranda et Notanda, 160
Agrippa, Cornelius, 89
Alexander III., a ghost at the wedding festivities of, 23
Alive, a man buried, 111
Annandale, strange apparitions in, 224
Angus, the Earl of, bewitched, 58
Animals buried alive, 99, 101
"Ane Interlude of the Laying of a Gaist," 150
Angels, a girl conversing with, 155
Apparitions, *Recueil de Dissertations sur les*, 22
Apparitions, 124, 143, 167, 169
Arran, Earl and Countess of, 83
Arran, causing storms at, 133
Argyle, the Earl of, supposed to be aided by a witch, 82; Coming from Holland, 167
Astonishing apparitions in the reign of Charles II., 143
Athole, Earl of, crowned with red-hot iron, 32
Athole, Countess of, accused of practising the *black art*, 43; Curious letter from, 44
Athole-men addicted to music, 135
Aubrey's life of Dr. Kettle, 213
Aubrey's *Miscellanies*, 120
Bagpipes considered ungodly, 135
Ballantyne, Sir Lewis, raising the devil, 49
Balmerino, Lord, gets an amatorious potion, 49

Balfour, Alison, an Orcadian witch, 84
Balcarras, Lord, sees the ghost of his friend, 170
Balgarran's, the laird of, daughter, 171
Barker, Janet, convicted at Edinburgh, 113
Bathgate, Elizabeth, pursued for sorcery, 107
Baxter's *World of Spirits*, 218, 219
Beaumont's *Treatise of Spirits*, 214, 217
Bell's *Treatise of Witchcraft*, 173, 209, 217
Bell's *Trial of Witchcraft*, 209
Bedford, R., murder of, at Leith, 92
Benoit, a wizard of Berne, 35
Bible, the, and the ghost, 150
Birrell's account of the murder of Warriston, 90
Bishops said to be cloven-footed, 146
Blackadder, John, 145
Blind Harry's account of an apparition, 25
Blood rained at Camelon, 20
Boots, the torture of the, 64
Boquhane, the Laird of, 54
Bothwell, the Earl of, a noted necromancer, 79
Brightly, Rev. John, visions appearing to, 201
Broken on the wheel, 91
Bruce, King Robert, 29
Bruce's sermons, 80
Brugh, John, worried at a stake, 112
Bryson, Margaret, condemned and executed, 126

Buccleuch, Lady, addicted to witchcraft, 42
Buchanan on the murder of Darnley, 42
Burne, Nicol, declares Knox a sorcerer, 48
Burning animals alive, 210
Burying animals alive, 210
Butter, making enchanted figures of, 53
Caithness, very singular case at, 180
Camelon, wonderful visions at, 20
Cameron, Bishop of Glasgow, mysterious death of, 33
Caps, peculiar, of the 17th century, 212
Caratake, King, 17, 18
Cazotte's *Diable Amoureux*, 35
Cattle, destruction of, 98
Charles I., King, death of predicted, 120
Charles II., King, numerous cases during the reign of, 126
Chaunerie, C. Ross burned at, 53
Child-birth, increasing the pain of, 43
Civil war predicted, 120
Clay images, making, for shooting at, 52
Clelland's *Effigies Clericorum*, 22.
Closeburn, curious case at, 161
Cochrane, Sir John, 167
Cock, Janet, accused of making persons go mad, 128
Corrichie, the skirmish of, 50
Cotta's *Tryall of Witchcraft*, 106
Cool's, the Laird of, ghost, 205
Cornfoot, Janet, brutally murdered, 175
Craigmad, strange incident at, 145
Crieff, the Knock of, 159
Cromartie's, Lord, wedding, 88; his *Synopsis Apocalyptica*, 89
Crombie, Thomas, hanged at Dalkeith, 112
Crosford, apparitions at, 167
Cullen, Lord, 172
Cumyn, the Red, death of, and strange prophecy, 29

Cunningham, John, *alias* Doctor Fian, 55
Curing stone, the Lee Penny, 100
Curates said to be wizards, 147
Dalkeith, incidents at, 110, 112, 131
Dalyell, General, the death of, 147
Dalyell's *The Darker Superstitions of Scotland*, 261
Dancing, 137
Death, precognition of, 124, 125, 214
Devil's, the, mark, 113
Devil, the, in the likeness of a man, 131; Likeness of a brown dog, 132; The singing of, 134
Devilish charms, 216
Dew, bloody, 38
Dickie's *The Philosophy of Witchcraft*, 262
Digby, Sir Kenelm, 81
Dickson, John, preaching near Glasgow, 144
Diseases transferred from one person to another, 45
Don, the river, a monster seen in, 120
Dorchester, spirit manifestations at, 225
Dornoch, an execution at, 200
Douglas, Lady, penurious disposition of, 150
Dreams revealing the haunts of the hillmen, 147
Drummond, Alex., suffered death for sorcery, 101
Duffus, King, dangers from witchcraft, 21
Duffus, Lord, 207
Dunbar's *The Dream of the Abbot*, 40
Duncane, Geillis, 56
Dumfriesshire, remarkable revelations at, 160
Dunce, wonderful visions at, 203
Dundas, Robert, King's advocate, 184
Dundee, Viscount, the ghost of, 170
Dunnottar Castle, 138

INDEX.

Du Rosset's *Histoires Tragiques*, 37
Duns, witchcraft at, 220
East Barnes, witchcraft at, 98
East Lothian, witches at, 260
Eastwood, a woman *delated* at, 97
Echard's *History*, 123
Eden-Hall, drinking glass at, 22
Edinburgh Castle, apparitions at, 169
Elfland, Queen of, 52
Egg, an enchanted, 107
Elgin wonder, the, 201
Escheat, the gift of, 128
Eyemouth, sorcery at, 106
Fairies, disappearance of, 22
Familiar spirits, 217
Females in masculine attire, 218
Fian, Doctor, and his associates, 55; Trial, and confession of, 64; Burned to death, 72
Fiddlers, difficulty of getting sober, 136
Fife, many witches in the coast side of, 112
Flodden Field, prodigies announcing the fate of, 38
Forfar, witchcraft in, 256
Forres, burning of witches at, 21
Forrester, Rev. Thomas, of Alva, 166
Foullis, Lady, indicted for witchcraft, 52
Fountainhall, Lord, 207
France, witchcraft in, 106
Fraser, James, of Alness, 183
Fraser, Janet, singular incident, 161
Fraser's *Discourse of the Second Sight*, 143, 259
Fynnie, Agnes, the indictment of, 113
Galgacus, King, precognition of defeat, 18
Gardner, Rev. John, minister of Elgin, 201
Gentlewoman, a, infested by an evil spirit, 36
Giffard's *Dialogue concerning Witches and Witchcraft*, 210, 212

Gifford, Hugh, Lord of Yester, 24
Glammis, Lady, trial and execution, 38
Glasgow, amusing circumstance at, 136; Strange sights near, 144
Gordon, Lady Anne, going in male attire, 147
Gourock, 131
Gowrie, the Earl of, addicted to magic, 87
Graves, numerous and unaccountable, 159
Greave, Thomas, burned for curing diseases, 97
Greenock, 131
Grierson, Isabel, convicted of witchcraft and burned, 95
Haddington, a witch at, 58
Hallow-Even, charms at, 97
Halriud-House, 59
Hamilton, Sir Alex., pulled out of bed by witches, 45
Hamiltoun, Sir James, death of, 40
Hattaraick, Alex., a celebrated wizard, 105
Henry I., King, presents a fairy's cup, 22
Hibbert's *Description of Shetland*, 256
Hidden treasure, the search for, 120
Hilton, witchcraft at, 106
Hobgoblin Hall, 24
Hollingshed, R., 17, 20, 35, 36
Holland's, Lord, daughters, precognition of death, 124; Daughters at Oxford, 213
"Holocaust," the, a poem, 261
Hume of Godscroft, 73
Hutcheson, Margaret, lybelled, 127
Hutchison, Margaret, invests a man with the pains of child-bed, 45
Huntly, Earl of, unaccountable death, 50
Huntly, Countess of, patroness of witches, 50
Incubi and Succubi, 34
Inchbrakie, the family of, 159

Innerkip, witches at, 130
Iona, celebrated witch at, 18
Irish-men, addicted to music, 135
Irvine, trial for witchcraft at, 255
James I., death prophesied by a witch, 30
James IV. and the apparition, 38
James V., executions in the reign of, 38; Strange dreams of, 40
James VI., his dæmonologie, 86, 255
Jardine, Sir Alex., of Applegirth, 149
Kennedy, Sir Arch., the devil carries away, 148
Kenneth, King, laws against wizards, 20
Kettle, Dr., and Lord Holland's daughters, 213
Kilernan, the parish of, 181; Witches at, 261
Killicranky, the battle of, 170
Kincaid, John, strangled by his wife, 90
Kinross, remarkable event at, 177
Kirkcudbrightshire, singular doings of a spirit in, 229
Kirk, Rev. R., on the witch mark, 209
Kirk's *Secret Commonwealth*, 131, 135, 256
Kirkpatrick, Roger, of Closeburn, 29
Kirkpatrick, Sir Thomas, 230
Kirktown of Auchterarder, 101
Kirkton's *History*, 158
Knox, John, account of strange dreams, 40; Accounted a wizard, 47
Knox's *The First Blast of the Trumpet against the Monstrous Regiment of Women*, 48
Knox, Robert, account of witchcraft at Pollock, 138
Lamb, Dr., torn to pieces, 176
Lamont, Mary, the confession of, 131
Lamps, magical, 28
Lanark, strange sights at, 167

Lasswade, an instance at, 103
Last execution of a witch in Scotland, 199
Lauder, Margaret, convicted at Edinburgh, 113
Lauderdale, Duke of, on witchcraft incidents, 219
Languages, speaking numerous, 222
Lawrie, Patrick, burned for sorcery, 94
Lee, Sir Charles, daughter of, 213
Lee, the Laird of, 99
Lee Penny curing stone, 100
Lesley, General, an apparition of, 123
Lilly's Life, 120
Lindsay, Sir James, death of, 29
Lindsay, Sir David, *The Abbasse*, 48
Linlithgow Loch, the swans at, 125
Loth, the parish of, 199
Lothian, Earl of, worried by a wizard, 46
Loudun nuns, 226
Macalrean, Euphame, confession of, 58, 72
Macbeth and the weird sisters, 21
MacGilchrist, John, town-clerk of Glasgow, 171
Macgillimondan, Wm., a warlock, 53
M'Grigor, Donald, a child of, bewitched, 152
Mackenzie's, Sir George, blood issuing from, 148
Mackenzie, Sir George, words of, 94, 126, 262
Macleod's *History of Witches*, 260
Mar, Earl of, practising magic, 34
Mar, loud tucking of drums heard in, 120
Mark, the family of, 45
Mary, Queen, reign fruitful of witchcraft, 41
Maxwell, Henry, of Dalswinton, 165
Mid-Calder, witchcraft, 195
Miller, Mrs., of Kilmaurs, 174

INDEX.

Mitchell, Wm., the mad tinklerian doctor, 195
Mitchell's *The Philosophy of Witchcraft*, 262
Mogul, King, conspiracy against him, 18
Moncrieff's *The Poor Man's Physician*, 130
Montgomerie, Wm., of Caithness, 182
Montgomery, Captain Alex., *A Lady's Lamentation*, 122
Montrose, Marquis of, guided by prophecies, 122
Monzie, witchcraft at, 151
Moray, Lady, precognition of death, 171
Munro, Hector, indicted for witchcraft, 52
Mylne, Margaret, seen in the likeness of a cat, 128
Napier, Barbara, 72, 73
Napier, Sir Archibald, deemed a wizard, 121
Napier, Sir Robert, precognition of death, 124
Natholocus, King, witchcraft in the time of, 18
Newbigging, 103
New England, sorcery at, 174
Nicniven, a sorceress burned at St. Andrews, 51
Nicolson, Michael Stewart, 130
Nin-Gilbert, Margaret, confession of, 182
Nisbet, Alie, suffers death for witchcraft, 106
Niven, Catherine, burned at Crieff, 159
Nues, Margaret, a witch, 45
Ochiltree, Lord, the daughter of, 48
Orkney, the Earl of, 84
Orkney, trials at, 255
Ormiston, Lady, 106
Osborne's *Traditional Memorials*, 120
Osborne, Luke, and his wife, 176
Oswald, Catherine, indictment of, 102

Paisley, five witches burned at, 172
Paterson's *Belief in Witchcraft*, 260
Patrick, Saint, assailed by witches, 19
Pear, the enchanted, of Coalston, 24
Pearson, A., convicted of sorcery, 52
Peden, life of, 168
Pepper-milne burne, 103
Perth, curious circumstances at, 125
Peterhead, mysterious sounds at, 120
Pin, testing by insertion of, 105, 113, 194
Pins in a wizard's head, 65
Pinet, a wizard, 36
Pitcairn's *Criminal Trials*, 262
Pittenweem, the witches of, 175, 259
Poltrot de Meré, 30
Prynne's *Hidden Works of Darkness*, 218
Queensberry, Duke of, 148
Ramsay, Davy, clockmaker, 120
Ramsay's *Astrologia Restaurata*, 120
Ramsay, Isabel, getting a sixpence from the devil, 127
Reid, James, convicted of sorcery, 94
Reid, John, strangled at Paisley, 172
Renfrewshire, witchcraft at, in 1677, 138
Renfrewshire, the witches in 1697, 171, 257
Renfrewshire, origin of the manufacture of thread at, 174
Rigwoody witch, the, 177
Ring-Croft of Stocking, 230, 257
Ring with a death's head, 170
Ross, Christian, burned for making clay images, 53
Ross, Captain David, of Little Dean, 199
Rothes, Duke of, 147
Roy, Bessy, trial for witchcraft, 54

Royalists supposed to be in the service of Satan, 146
Rutherford, Wm., vision revealed to, 203
Rutherglen, 144
St. Andrews, a notable witch burned at, 51
St. Catherine's, 103
Sampson, Agnes, trial and confession, 59, 75
Satan appearing in the form of a *medicinar*, 105
Salton Wood, the devil raised in, 106
Sandy's travels, 148
Sandilands, Patrick, son of Lord Torphichen, 194
Scalcraig, strange visions at, 202
Scribonius, 37
Scott, T., Justice-Clerk, 41
Scott of Scotstarvet, 49
Scott, Sir Michael, a celebrated enchanter, 27
Scottish countess eloped with a band of gipsies, 122
Scott's *Discovery of Witchcraft*, 50, 261
Scrabster in Caithness, 181
Second sight, 251, 260
Shaw, Christian, the case of, 171, 256
Shetland, trials at, 256
Ship endangered by an Incubus, 34
Showers of bonnets, hats, and guns, 167
Sickness laid beneath a barn door, 210
Simson, Arch., minister of Dalkeith, 46
Sinclair's *Satan's Invisible World*, 134, 256
Soulis, Lord, boiled to death, 27, 28
Spalding, James, buried alive, 111
Spedlins, the tower of, a ghost story, 149
Spott, many witches burned at, 176

Spynie, Lord, letter to Lindsay, 75
Statutes against witchcraft repealed, 200
Stewart, John, master of Orkney, 84, 85
Stewart, Wm., hanged for sorcery, 52
Succubi and Incubi, 34, 36
Telfair's *True Relation of an Apparition*, 230, 257
Tetragrammaton, the word, 88
Tinklerian doctor, the mad, 195
Thomas the Rhymer, 23
Torthorwald, Lord, assassinated, 83
Torphichen, Lord, the son of, bewitched, 194
Thurso, trial of Margaret Nin-Gilbert, 191
Tranent, witchcraft at, 56
Transported through the air, 207
Traquaire, Earl of, 111
Wallace, Margaret, executed for curing and inflicting diseases, 97
Walker, Patrick, vindication of Mr. Cameron, 137
Wax images, witchcraft by means of, 21, 31
Weems, Rev. John, minister of Duns, 220
Westminster Abbey, 120
Whirlwind, prophesying a, 129
"Whistle o'er the lave o't," 136
Wilkie, Rev. John, preaching on witchcraft, 195
Witch marks, 87, 208, 209
"Witty and entertaining exploits of George Buchanan," 175
Woodrow mentions two *Remarkables*, 125; *Analecta*, 262; Letter to, 181
Worried at a stake and burned, 112, 119
Young, Isobel, indictment of, 98

www.ingramcontent.com/pod-product-compliance
Lightning Source LLC
Chambersburg PA
CBHW022054160426
43198CB00008B/233